FROM FOREST FARM TO SAWMILL

SHUXUAN ZHOU

FROM FOREST FARM TO SAWMILL

Stories of Labor, Gender, and the Chinese State

University of Washington Press / Seattle

From Forest Farm to Sawmill was made possible in part by a grant from the China Studies Program, a division of the Henry M. Jackson School of International Studies at the University of Washington.

This book will be made open access within three years of publication thanks to Path to Open, a program developed to bring about equitable access and impact for the entire scholarly community, including authors, researchers, libraries, and university presses around the world. Learn more at https://about.jstor.org/path-to-open/.

Design by Mindy Basinger Hill

Composed in Minion Pro

Photographs by the author unless otherwise noted.

UNIVERSITY OF WASHINGTON PRESS   *uwapress.uw.edu*

LIBRARY OF CONGRESS CATALOGING-IN-PUBLICATION DATA
Names: Zhou, Shuxuan, 1987– author.
Title: From forest farm to sawmill : stories of labor, gender, and the
    Chinese state / Shuxuan Zhou.
Description: Seattle : University of Washington Press, [2024] |
    Includes bibliographical references and index.
Identifiers: LCCN 2023051400 | ISBN 9780295752662 (hardback) |
    ISBN 9780295752679 (paperback) | ISBN 9780295752686 (ebook)
Subjects: LCSH: Lumber trade—Employees—Relocation—China—
    History. | Labor policy—China—History. | Employee rights—China. |
    Occupational mobility—China. | Tree farmers—China—Interviews. |
    Sawmill workers—China—Interviews.
Classification: LCC HD9766.C62 Z54 2024 | DDC 338.1/7498—dc23/
    eng/20240410
LC record available at https://lccn.loc.gov/2023051400

TO ALL RAGING *nainai* AND *popo*

CONTENTS

PREFACE

It was 1997, and I was ten years old. The music video of the song "Start Over" pervaded every Chinese government-owned television channel. A storm disrupts the celebration of a group of factory workers. An angry father and a melancholic mother chase a running boy into the pouring rain. As they follow him into an abandoned factory building, the vocalist passionately sings: "If your heart can keep on dreaming, the world's still full of love. Whether you succeed or fail, you've just gotta start over."[1] At that time, I didn't know that this song was a forecast of a nationwide policy storm that would force my family to start over mentally and financially.

On February 15, 1999, a sketch titled *Cheer Up* was featured in the Chinese Central Television Lunar New Year Gala, still the world's most-watched TV show and one that reflects the Chinese Communist Party's perspective and agenda. In this sketch, a male state enterprise worker proudly declared: "Workers need to think for the state. Let us embrace the layoffs!"[2] That year, the state-owned sawmill near the city of Shaowu in the forested southeastern province of Fujian, where my family had worked for decades, had started privatizing and laying off workers.

In 2000, all three thousand workers at the mill, including my father and several extended family members, were laid off. We moved to the big city of Xiamen on the coast, over four hundred kilometers away, so that my father could search for a new job. I left for college in Beijing and later migrated to Seattle for graduate school.

After 2000, laid-off state workers were represented in mainstream culture by two contrasting stereotypes: some were lazy, incompetent, passive, and a burden to the Chinese economy, while others successfully "started over," adjusting to the new norms of the job market—reduced pay, long hours, no benefits, and an abusive hierarchy.[3]

Aiming to present a more diverse and nuanced view of the experiences of laid-off workers and families, I began interviewing former Shaowu Sawmill workers in 2008. My interviewees at that time mostly agreed with the state-promoted narrative that the state workers had selflessly sacrificed their careers to help save the Chinese national economy from its socialist past, guided by the "universal" capitalist remedies of development, efficiency, and competition.

On a steamy summer day in 2011, I sat in the cramped apartment of my *waipo* (maternal grandmother). Trying to keep the apartment cool, she had put the shades on the windows and kept the lights off, leaving just one kitchen window open so that she could see to cook. Waipo too had worked at the sawmill, and she was the first forestry worker I interviewed from the generation of workers hired in the 1960s—the parents of the laid-off workers. She resisted my attempts to ask her about the experience of migrating to and working at the Shaowu Sawmill. Instead she told me a life story, seemingly recited from a script about twenty-five minutes long, in chronological order and filled with the tales of suffering I had heard from her hundreds of times as I was growing up. No matter how I framed my questions, she stuck to this narrative, replying "How can I remember that?" and returning to the script. Interviewing her frustrated me, and I stopped trying. I left my camcorder on, and for a few days I just watched her silently through the monitor, feeling exhausted and trapped in this close, hot space with someone who I felt did not want to have an "honest" conversation with me.

One day, as Waipo was working in the kitchen, plodding about slowly (probably because of chronic knee problems), my camera captured a silhouette of her moving in the light, like a contemporary dancer or drama performer under the stage lights. In this image, Waipo took center stage.

Seeing Waipo in this unusual light prompted me to question my approach. Had I ever viewed her and other forestry laborers as protagonists in China's recent history? Or was I only trying to portray them as victims of the "China miracle?" Would centering their lives and labor in the recent history of Chinese forestry influence my understanding of the transitions

Still image from video of my grandmother working in the kitchen.

in this industry? Watching my grandmother's strength through the camera monitor became one of the defining moments in my research.

In the following years, I expanded my interviews to include various groups of laborers in the forestry and wood-processing industries: not only more sawmill workers from multiple generations, but also workers on state forest farms, peasants who owned and managed forests, and rural migrant workers now working in privately owned timber businesses. The hundreds of people I talked to over more than a decade asked pertinent questions about the effects of privatization on Chinese forests, workers, economy, and society: Why were the workers the ones who were "sacrificed"? Was their sacrifice necessary to China's economic rise? What enabled private timber businesses to succeed in the twenty-first century? Didn't the workers who built the state enterprises deserve part of the proceeds from sales of their land and assets? Which was better for the forests, capitalist privatization or socialist collectivization?

All these questions pushed me to reframe my research questions. No longer did I simply seek to document how the workers had survived the privatization of the forestry and timber industry—that is, how the economic miracle had left them behind. I now asked a broader question: How did these workers' labor and the economic (as well as social and ecological) value they created help to enable China's economic miracle? When the state "started over" during its transition from socialism to state capitalism, and when it forced the workers to start over by taking away their jobs and livelihoods, what was passed down and accumulated, for both the state and the workers, and what was lost?

ACKNOWLEDGMENTS

Having grown up in a working-class family in which I was discouraged from reading books that would not directly contribute to better scores in my school exams, I underestimated the type and amount of labor involved in writing a book. This project turned out to be a struggle-filled and humbling journey. Yet I thank the naivete and optimism of my twentysomething self, because this journey directed me back to the community I was born into. When I was a child, my parents, extended family, and community members all told me that I needed to do well in school so that I could leave my community. I fulfilled their wish: high school, college, and graduate school took me farther and farther away from my place of origin. However, life has a sense of irony. My "doing well in school" resulted in my starting this research project in graduate school and rejoining my community to study things that I grew up with, yet knew little about. At the end of this writing journey, my understanding of my community and the role my people play in the economy and society has fundamentally changed, as has my perception of the politicization and orientation of the labor movement.

Many people accompanied, supported, and encouraged me in this journey. The storytellers—the *nainai* (grandma), *popo* (grandma), and *ayi* (auntie)—generously shared their memories with me, forcefully or timidly told me about their experiences and views, and kindly passed down intergenerational wisdom about fighting against injustice. In the sawmill community where I grew up, northerners like to be called *nainai*, and southerners like to be called *popo*. (These terms are also used as respectful forms of address for older women in general.) Many of them have passed away since our interviews, and none of them read English. I am deeply grateful to the women who inspired this book and yet won't be able to read it.

Among those who told me about their life and labor histories are members of my own family. I feel lucky to have spent time with my maternal grandmother, my *waipo*, because of this book. I thank Waipo for insisting on telling her story to me in her own way and for tolerating my impatience and misunderstanding when I was interviewing her and yet not truly listening to her. My parents were unsure where my book was going and worried about my publicly expressing opinions that are critical of authoritarian power, but they supported me anyway, contributing their memories, connections, and materials to my research.

My persistence in this project owes much to my scholarly mentors and friends. Sasha Su-Ling Welland taught and continuously demonstrates how feminist scholars ground our works in the ways women, queer, and other silenced and oppressed groups theorize their own worlds. Because of Sasha's trust, I dared to dream about writing a book. Priti Ramamurthy oriented me toward the connections between economic structures and entangled feelings and relationships. Steve Harrell read every draft of my manuscript (there were so many!) and boosted my confidence in owning my argument even when it's controversial. Shana Ye was the best comrade with whom to navigate a prolonged book-revision process. I'm grateful for Xin Huang's and Lin Li's respectively calm and cheerful styles of affirmation. alma khasawnih had the most effective pep talk for pulling me out of my self-doubt. I also thank Tong Xin, Shi Hongmei, Ann Anagnost, Daniel Abramson, Jacob Eyferth, Susan Whiting, Silvia Federici, and Yomi Braester for their curiosity about the stories I wanted to tell and for helping me develop a voice with which to tell them.

I also had the good luck to present portions of this project at various symposiums and conferences where I received valuable feedback and made friendships that continue to this day: the Michigan-Fudan Gender Studies Dissertation Workshop, facilitated by Wang Zheng, Lisa Rofel, and Deborah Rosenfelt; the Feminist Studies Dissertation Workshop, facilitated by Amanda Lock Swarr; the China Anthropology Group, organized by Steve Harrell, where I reflected on my fieldwork stories alongside Darren Byler and Gladys Jian; the Chinese History Writing Workshop, facilitated by Madeleine Yue Dong, where I wrote with Qian He and Xiaoshun Zeng; the symposium "Engendering Social Transformation in China," organized by

Feng Yuan, Guoguang Wu, and Helen Lansdowne; the conference "Towards a Global History of Primitive Accumulation," organized by Pepijn Brandon and Niklas Frykman; and the National Women's Studies Association annual conferences, where Wenjie Liao and Charlie Zhang befriended me and have had to field random questions from me about my book ever since.

I had the privilege of having my institutional homes at the Department of Gender, Women and Sexuality Studies at the University of Washington and the Graduate School of East Asia Studies at the Freie Universität Berlin, which provided me with time, space, funding, and intellectual communities. Research grants from the Association for Asian Studies, the Bridges Center for Labor Studies, the Chiang Ching-kuo Foundation for International Scholarly Exchange, and the Simpson Center for the Humanities made possible my research, thinking, and writing.

Lorri Hagman has been an important and patient advocate of the book throughout its multiple transformations. Caitlin Tyler-Richards and Joeth Zucco shepherded the publication process and were receptive to my ideas and preferences. Several anonymous readers gave insightful feedback that improved the manuscript. Claire Allen, Teresa Nemeth, and Erika Bűky edited my manuscript, helped tighten my prose, and pushed for clarity that would make the work accessible to general readers.

I would have not been able to write this book without childcare support from Rui-Hua Li, Phyllis Edwards, teachers at ReWA Early Learning Center and the Beacon Hill Elementary School, and most importantly, my life partner, Aaron Hartwell. Aaron's steady and empathetic company was there throughout every twist and turn of my book-writing journey, and his indulging love permitted me to use all my paid time off from my day job over the past four years to revise my manuscript (which is not just for myself and my family). My gratitude, as always, goes to my child Wren, this time for wisely telling me, "You don't have to publish the book. You can just print it out, and I will read it."

FROM FOREST FARM TO SAWMILL

INTRODUCTION

ACCUMULATING CAPITAL, ACCUMULATING KNOWLEDGE

The Wuyi mountain range in northern Fujian was hot and humid as usual in the summer of 2018. We drove from Shaowu city, turning off the highway onto winding roads through rolling hills covered with pine trees, firs, and bamboo. The road followed a river alongside a mossy cliff. The temperature dropped several degrees, and the air we breathed felt lighter. Then the road forked: a muddy road led to Dragon Lake Village, but we took a paved road over a bridge to the Dragon Lake State Forest Farm. Dogs napped in the shade. Grasshoppers the size of mice were camouflaged in the flowering green bushes, and spiders crawled through the gaps under the wooden window frames of the farm offices.

What is now the quiet office area of the state forest farm was once a bustling state logging camp that provided logs to sixteen Chinese provinces via the Shaowu State Sawmill, located in the city. The camp was built in the late 1950s and improved and expanded through the 1980s.[1] Many workplace accidents happened in the camp in the 1960s: falling trees killed loggers, and trucks full of logs ran into the river. After a rash of accidents, the manager hired a feng shui master, who attributed them to the removal of a small hill in the middle of the camp in the late 1950s. The removal broke the natural geomancy of "five dragons playing with a pearl" — five big mountains encircling a small hill — and thus brought misfortune upon the foresters. Advised by the master, they built a round red pavilion to replace the missing hill, and workplace accidents dropped off.

After nearly fifty years of timber harvesting and cultivation, in the early

2000s, local forests were recategorized as "ecological public welfare forests," and the farm was reoriented toward conservation.[2] Commercial logging was largely banned, and most of the permanent state employees were laid off. The logging camp that had employed a thousand workers in its heyday in the 1960s and '70s was reduced to just sixty employees charged with administrative and patrolling tasks.

The farm began hiring seasonal migrant workers from rural areas in Yunnan and Guizhou to cultivate and thin the trees. Unlike the previous state forest farm employees, who were entitled to state-funded housing and other social benefits, the new seasonal workers lived in temporary hand-built sheds or in abandoned state farm or village houses and often worked without formal contracts or employee benefits.

Ten former forest farm workers accompanied me to the Dragon Lake Forest Farm for my last round of a decade of interviews with state forestry workers. Those ten workers agreed that the changes in forestry were worth writing about. "You look around. There are no people here now," one reflected, ignoring the new migrant laborers who were taking care of or felling trees in the mountains. "The houses are run down, and it is even more rural here than in the villages. Looking at this, who could recall the prominence of our state forestry industry?"

In 2013, together with several former Shaowu State Sawmill workers, then in their fifties, I watched electric welders dismantling a fallen ten-story gantry crane during the demolition of the mill. (A gantry crane, designed for lifting and moving heavy objects, consists of a beam bridging two trestles that run on tracks). The sawmill workers echoed the forest farm workers' sorrow and anger about being forgotten, along with their pride in the value their labor had created. They proudly recalled how the cranes had been built by the previous generation of workers in the 1960s: "They piled up the logs and stood on top of the pile to weld the metal strips together. As they piled the logs higher and higher, the welded metal strips grew taller and taller to the height of ten stories. There was no equipment like a lift to assist—they did all the piling, climbing, and welding solely relying on their own bodies."

The state sawmill was privatized around 2000 and divided into four pieces, which were sold to four private wood-processing companies. All the workers lost their jobs. The four companies moved their mills to other places in 2012, and the remaining building and facilities were demolished. The workers recounted the demolition process with anguish: "Two months ago, they blew up our chimneys. Today they came to demolish the cranes. They will take the train track next. Our mill will be truly gone then."

These workers' grief, anger, and longing to be remembered stood out in the stories they told me when I interviewed them between 2008 and 2018. These emotions became even more evident when the workers came together to take collective action against the local government, two of which are documented in this book. They resisted being forgotten and deemed "irrelevant" to today's China.

The forestry workers' anxiety and anger speak against the broader recent discourse about the Chinese economy, which overlooks their contributions to it and to Chinese society. According to a commonly accepted narrative in China and elsewhere, the Maoist era (from 1949 through the late 1970s), dominated by class struggle and cultural revolution, caused chaos in Chinese society and stagnation in the economy. Reforms initiated by Deng Xiaoping in the late 1970s stimulated the economy and pulled the Chinese people out of poverty. It is true that China has astonished the world with its rapid economic growth since the 2010s. But a big reason for the astonishment is the assumption that the Chinese state and Chinese capitalist entrepreneurs began accumulating capital from ground zero in the late twentieth century.

By disconnecting Maoism from post-Maoism, and erasing the contributions of the older generation of workers to the post-Mao economy, this narrative prevents us from seeing the trajectory of economic development and labor politics in China. It justifies the capitalist appropriation of the assets created by these older workers. It also legitimizes labor exploitation under state capitalism by positing the capitalist market economy and its presumed trickle-down benefits as the means of saving the Chinese economy and people from the economic stagnation and social chaos of the Maoist era. Furthermore, because people who are concerned about labor oppression in China focus mainly on rural migrant workers in the post-1980 market economy, the earlier workers' oppression and resistance during China's transition from socialism to state capitalism becomes doubly invisible: intentionally silenced by the state and capitalist entrepreneurs and overlooked by scholars and activists.

The forestry workers' stories inspired me to look at the history of China's forestry industry through the lens of capital accumulation and to see how their labor under socialism accumulated value for today's capitalist economy. Their stories thus serve as a thread linking Chinese economic and political history from Maoist state socialism to post-Mao state capitalism (from the 1980s to the present), revealing the continuities and disjunctions of economic development, capital accumulation, and labor politics across these two periods. These stories prompt two sets of interrelated questions. First, what has or has not changed as ownership of the means of production, uses of labor, and accumulation of capital in the Fujian lumber industry has moved from state to private control? Second, how have workers understood their roles and life changes in the context of transformations in the forestry industry, the Chinese economy, and capital accumulation? How has their evolving view of life changes and their structural causes shaped their oppositional consciousness and actions?

Capital Accumulation in Chinese Forestry

In Marxist theory, *capital* is defined as accumulated money, goods, and assets that are available and ready for further circulation, reinvestment, and production to create more capital. As Karl Marx himself observed, capital "preserves and perpetuates itself in and through circulation."[3] Accumulation is intrinsic to capital. When business profits, goods, and constructed assets — which can include equipment, machinery, buildings, and land — are reinvested into the economy, the sum of capital increases. This is the process of *capital accumulation*.

Capital accumulation in Chinese forestry has taken two primary forms: expropriation and exploitation. *Expropriation* happens when land, assets, resources, and human labor are confiscated and conscripted into capital's circuits of self-expansion. This process usually involves the exercise of violence and regulatory intervention by the state. Expropriation results in the separation of laborers from their means of production, including land, resources, and infrastructure. After this separation, the laborers must sell their labor power to earn a wage. This necessity is the foundation for exploitation.

The entity that now owns the means of production purchases labor power with a wage and uses that labor power to create a product. When the owner of the means of production pays the laborer less than the full value of that product (i.e., extracts surplus value and invests that value in the capital circuits to create more profits), *exploitation* occurs.

Expropriation sets up the stage for exploitation. Expropriation often takes place in the early stages of an economy, or during economic crises or fundamental transitions when the economy needs to enlist exterior labor and exterior means of production. This is why Marx referred to this stage as the *original* (often translated as "primitive") accumulation of capital.[4]

Capital accumulation occurred during significant transitions in Chinese forestry: the establishment of state socialism in the 1950s and its transformation into state capitalism beginning around 1980. The three key elements of capital in Chinese forestry are land, timber, and labor. Both economic transitions involved the expropriation of all three elements and reallocation of their ownership and usership to enable their exploitation: first by the state, and then by the state and private capitalists.

The Chinese Communist Party's socialist vision and the country's need for self-defense in the Cold War, along with the Soviet Union's example of industrialization under Stalin, led the leadership to prioritize heavy industry in the 1950s.[5] However, unlike the Soviet Union, which already had strong transport infrastructure, buildings, and machinery, China had a weak base for production. Therefore, the state used its massive supply of cheap labor to compensate for its small base of capital by setting up labor-intensive heavy industries, including forestry.

Operating according to Mao's proclamation that "humanity is destined to conquer nature," the socialist regime initiated massive projects that exploited natural resources in order to realize its vision of modernization and economic development.[6] Among these projects was the establishment of state forestry in Fujian in the 1950s and 1960s. Timber, which was used for railroad ties, pit props in mines, and construction frames, was a major resource for industrialization.

To establish the state forestry, the state confiscated land and properties from the bourgeoisie and private businesses in the 1950s. Rural land was collectivized and given to villages. The forests were also collectivized and owned by villages, but the villages were not allowed to commodify the timber in the forests. Only state enterprises had the authority and the means to do so. A state program moved twenty thousand peasants from the North China Plain into the Fujian mountains. These people developed the buildings and machinery for the state forestry enterprises from scratch, and these enterprises then monopolized logging, wood processing, and trade. Thus, through expropriations of land, timber, and labor, the state established forestry in China.

Once the labor and means of production were in place, the forestry enterprises, like other state-owned industries, maximized capital accumulation through centralized allocation of labor and resources. The central planning system consistently channeled the products and profits back into production through two major mechanisms. First, the state suppressed consumption by controlling the prices of goods and compensating labor through localized coupon systems to create a cash scarcity. The lack of expenditure on infrastructure unrelated to production, moreover, gave individuals few opportunities for spending.[7] Heavy industry output could thus be funneled back into the production process to increase total production capacity and available capital.[8] Second, partly because consumption was limited, and labor and resources were controlled by the state, wages could be kept low. In sum, the socialist state accumulated capital by expropriating the means of production, exploiting labor, and exercising complete control over the flows of capital.[9]

In the 1980s and 1990s, as China turned gradually from state socialism to state capitalism, the state layered market activities on top of a planned economy: private enterprises grew, while state enterprises gradually lost dominance. In the late 1990s and early 2000s, as China entered the World Trade Organization, the state-owned sector was significantly downsized and privatized, and tens of millions of state workers were laid off. A domestic capitalist class thrived on the appropriation of former state assets (by taking them away from the state workers) and exploitation of a working class that consisted mostly of rural migrants.[10] Public property as a share of national wealth dropped from 70 percent in 1978 to 30 percent in around 2005. Since then the balance of state and private ownership has stabilized.[11]

State ownership is concentrated in capital-intensive sectors (such as steel, oil, petrochemicals, automobiles, rail, energy, telecommunications, and banking), while private ownership prevails in labor-intensive industries (including food production, textiles, services, information technology, retail sales, and manufacturing, including wood processing). The state's role in capital accumulation thus relies more on owning assets than on employing labor. Starting in the 1990s, different levels of government made it easier to expropriate rural land for private real-estate development. Rural land consolidation was legalized in the following decade.[12] China now has a mixed economy in which the state and private enterprises are both important drivers of capital accumulation. The state agencies act like capitalists, owning large enterprises and competing with each other and with private capital, and the state can also use its legal and administrative power to shape the trajectories of capital accumulation in the private sector.[13] Thus, China's political and economic system is a form of state capitalism.

In recent decades, there has also been a shift in the state's philosophical understanding of the relationship between humans and nature. From the 1980s onward, the Chinese central government initiated many reforestation and forest-conservation projects.[14] The floods that devastated central China in 1998 gave urgency to the idea of an "ecological civilization" and further immense reforestation projects. Starting with a few pilot projects in Fujian, the central government, acting on the idea that privatization could stop the state enterprises' excessive logging and increase the efficiency of forest management and uses, ordered the nationwide privatization of forest ownership and commodification.[15]

In southeastern China in the early years of the twenty-first century, forest usufruct was distributed to individual peasant households. The villages still collectively owned the land, but households could grow and harvest trees and sell the timber, as well as rent the land to others. When the peasants regained their rights to commodify timber, the state forest farms shifted away from logging and replanting trees to preserving the forests, and consequently most state workers lost their jobs. Thirteen farms in Shaowu that had once each employed six hundred to one thousand permanent workers now each employed just fifty to seventy administrators and patrollers. The farms hired southwestern rural migrants as seasonal and temporary contractors to cultivate and thin the trees. Simultaneously, the wood trade and processing market was opened to private enterprises. The state sawmills underwent full-scale privatization at the turn of the century, resulting in layoffs of all state workers.

These processes transferred the means of production (land, timber, and the assets created by the state workers) to capitalists (tree farmers and owners of wood-processing enterprises). The transfers amounted to expropriation endorsed by the state. The former state workers became a part of the new working class that could be exploited by the new capitalist class, and the capitalists increased their accumulation by exploitation when they hired migrant workers at low wages and without benefits.[16]

To fully understand capital accumulation in Chinese forestry, we need to explore two further questions. First, what facilitated the two rounds of expropriation of the means of production in the 1950s and the 1990s? Second, what policies did the state use to maximize the exploitation of which worker groups? Structural inequalities between urban and rural populations and between men and women are the keys to these inquiries.

Chinese people's lives in the Maoist era were conditioned by the rural and urban divide. After 1958, the household registration system severely restricted individual travel between rural and urban areas and made voluntary relocation virtually impossible. Generally speaking, urban land was owned by the state, while rural land was owned by the village collectives. Urban life was organized by *danwei* (work units), which usually revolved around a production or administrative unit, such as a factory, bureau, or school but also provided for the physical and social needs of the residents, including housing, education, child care, medical care, and recreation. Rural life, particularly productive labor (agriculture, construction, manufacturing, and other activities that produced goods for subsistence or trade), was collectivized.[17] Significantly more goods and resources were distributed to urban work units than to rural households.

China scholars have written much on the rural/urban division in Maoist China but little on the exceptions to this division. Although most work units were centered on industrial factories in urban areas, a variety of rural agricultural entities, which supported urban industrialization by providing food and raw materials, also established work units. These included state-owned forest farms, grain farms, and stud farms (for selective breeding of livestock), and the state sawmills. These work units were built on rural land, which was thus transformed physically and administratively into urban space. Similar entities included mines nationwide and national defense, technology, and basic industrial plants in the area known as the Third Front (a massive industrial development in interior northwestern and southwestern China that began in 1964).[18]

When members of peasant collectives were recruited to work on state farms, their migration from one rural area to another changed their social status and increased their access to food, goods, benefits, and infrastructure. The state provided the resources for laborers to build up their workplaces. In the middle of a landscape that was traditionally considered natural and rural, facilities such as logging camps had urban architecture and infrastructure, the workers received the same kinds of benefits as city people, and the land belonged to the state. The concrete buildings of the facility, including worker housing, were enclosed within walls, contrasting with the village residents' mud houses. Some of the mud paths outside the villages were paved to enable logging trucks to drive to town every day. Contrasting with the dark nights in a village lit only with oil lamps, the employee housing and shop floor (sited on village land) were brightly lit and powered by camp-owned electricity generators. Camp workers got more grain, oil, cotton fabric, and other rationed goods than villagers.

The state's control of cross-regional population flows, the segregation of urban and rural populations, and the drastic inequality in resource allocation were crucial to the mass mobilization of rural migrant laborers. Granting these migrants access to urban infrastructure and supplies while they lived in rural regions facilitated the state's expropriation of rural labor, land, and natural resources. Moreover, even though the forestry workers' living conditions were typically better than those they had left in their home villages or those in villages near the camp, their wages were still low, allowing the state to funnel the surplus value of their labor back into capital circulation and expansion.

Another dimension of structural difference—gender inequality—also facilitated labor exploitation. As many women as men worked in those forests. Most of the men were state workers with guaranteed salaries and full benefits. They felled trees, drove logging trucks, and worked with machinery in the mill. Most women were enrolled as "family dependent workers" (in the 1960s and 1970s) and "collective workers" (in the 1980s and 1990s) because they were wives and daughters of male state workers. Women tilled the land after logging, planted new trees, loaded products into railroad cars for shipping, stacked boards, and did other manual labor on the shop floor. They were treated as temporary workers and received less compensation. When the farms and mill were privatized, women were laid off first and received much less severance pay.

After privatization, when most of the jobs went to rural migrant workers from poorer southwestern provinces, the gendered division of labor was maintained, but in a different form. Both male and female workers were temporary hires who had no job security, no benefits, and low pay. The proportion of female workers was much smaller than before privatization. All women in this industry now were wives of the male workers, and they were in their forties and fifties. Younger women who had school-age children usually stayed in their home villages in southwestern China or worked on Shaowu's urban fringe. This was partly because there were no schools for migrant children around the logging camps and mills but also because there was no permanent housing available for seasonal migrant workers, as there was for the state workers.

Chinese forestry is not unique in using rural/urban and gender divisions as a means toward capital accumulation. Nor are these tactics confined to capitalism and socialism. Capitalism and colonialism have both relied on law and other instruments of state power to define women's work as nonwork and dispossess women of their labor, bodies, and assets.[19] Various socialist economies, by fiat, and capitalist economies, through market mechanisms, have also used the urban/rural and industrial/agricultural divides to facilitate the confiscation of land, goods, assets, and labor.[20]

The example of Chinese forestry blurs the boundary between socialism and capitalism, showing that both accumulate capital through dispossessing less powerful groups—rural people and women. Despite the dominant discourse in China that demarcates a major turning point between state socialism and state capitalism, the dichotomies of urban and rural, men and women, have continued to facilitate the expropriation of land, timber, labor, and industrial assets. Once established, these dichotomies were emphasized by creating proximity between the differentiated groups: placing an urban enterprise on rural land, and letting women work alongside men but registering them as nonworkers, facilitated the expropriation and exploitation of the less powerful groups. The example of the forestry industry shows that capital accumulation in state capitalist China has its roots in the socialist era: not only was the capital accumulated during the socialist era passed down and appropriated by the capitalist economy, but the systemic dualisms deployed to accumulate that capital were also perpetuated.

This book challenges the view that a complete break occurred between the Mao and post-Mao eras, the former devoted to class struggle and the latter to economic development.[21] It also challenges the conventional undervaluation of the legacies of women workers and peasants and the concealment of the operations of expropriation and exploitation in socialist China. And it strives to elevate the life stories of Chinese rural women—exploited because of both their rural origins and their gender—and shows these women's shifting feelings about, knowledge of, and responses to China's transitions.

Knowledge Accumulation among Forestry Laborers

While the state was promoting the process of capital accumulation over several decades, the workers were accumulating a different form of asset: knowledge and understanding of how their labor was being capitalized and how they could demand compensation. Their knowledge and feelings about their roles in the timber industry changed significantly over the decade and more of my fieldwork. Through these intertwined processes, they were transforming their accumulated knowledge and grievances into collective action.

My own process of knowledge accumulation began with interviewing sixteen women and collecting their life histories. From the sawmill, three of the interviewees were first-generation state workers, four were first-generation family dependent workers, one was a second-generation state worker, and four were second-generation collective workers. I also collected life histories from two first-generation family dependent workers at the forest farms and two peasants who lived near the farms. I identified and connected with these women through snowball sampling (past interviewees introducing me to new interviewees) and searches for women who came from different backgrounds (with respect to home provinces, positions, and post-layoff lives).

My use of women's narratives was inspired by feminist oral historians, who attempt to challenge the stereotypes within a dominant discourse by paying close attention to the voices of the underrepresented.[22] Each life history interview was two to four hours long.[23] I began with questions such as "Why and how did you come here?" and "Tell me about what happened to you in the past." After that, our conversations mostly followed interviewees' thoughts, and I limited myself to prompts asking for further detail or what happened next. These interviews enabled me to understand the women's work and life experiences and the forestry industry's changes from their own perspectives and frameworks. I have based the majority of my analysis on how these women narrators talked about their lives and Chinese history and economy.

Second, I conducted archival research at the Shaowu Forestry Department, Shaowu Sawmill, and Dragon Lake Forest Farm, and semistructured interviews with ten male former and current managers at these work units. These sources allowed me to identify specific periods and policies of particular significance in the development of the forestry. They also provided insights on the ideologies and rationales behind those initiatives, as well as how the policies and programs were implemented at the local and enterprise levels.[24]

Third, I spent a lot of time building (and rebuilding) relationships with the workers and peasants between 2008 and 2018. Most of my formal interviews took place in 2008, 2013, 2014, and 2018. I lived in the sawmill, forest farms, and villages for fourteen months between 2013 and 2014 and spent most of the following summers there until 2018. Casual and intentional conversations with the workers supplement my formal interviews, especially among those worker groups in which I was able to complete only one or two life history interviews. Informal conversations with other workers in the same group helped to fill in details related to work arrangements and experiences. Living at the forest farms also allowed me to observe interactions between state workers, migrant workers, and peasants.

The long duration of the study and my immersion in the workers' communities greatly shaped my research findings and the organization of this book. At the beginning, I encountered many women who rejected my interview requests by responding: "I'm illiterate. I don't know how to tell a story, and my story is not worth listening to." Even though these women, like my grandmother, had already narrated their stories of suffering to their families and communities for over half a century in a quest for material and emotional recognition, their internalized devaluation of their own work made them reluctant to talk with a researcher who was studying the forestry industry.

When I began my research, the workers tended to support the state's decisions regarding forestry reforms. Even though they also aired daily complaints about past and present difficulties in their lives, they did not attribute these difficulties to the policies. In later interviews and group conversations, however, I witnessed a notable increase in criticism of the treatment of workers during the reforms. This criticism ignited workers' collective oppositional actions. The collective actions in turn generated more criticism from workers about the nature of the state and about capitalists exploiting and dispossessing laborers in the forestry economy.

This book therefore not only analyzes structural oppression but also documents the transformations of workers' collective feelings and actions. As they saw themselves still exploited and their assets expropriated during the shift from state socialism to state capitalism, their feelings of grievance and anger accumulated. At first, their feelings showed up as complaints or criticism when they talked about life events. As time went by, their feelings evolved into critical and analytical knowledge of exploitation and expropriation as well as the skills and tactics they could use for individual and collective resistance.

Of course, the workers I interacted with were at different places along this spectrum of feeling, knowledge, and action. My analysis focuses primarily on those workers whose feelings had developed into critical knowledge and those who participated in collective actions, because it was their analysis of labor and dispossession in the forestry economy that inspired me to deploy the lens of capital accumulation. I use data collected from other interviews to supplement a narrator's individual life story in discussions of general working conditions and the impacts of reforms on women in the same group.[25]

The organization of the book seeks to reflect the progression from individual feeling to applied knowledge to collective action. Chapters 1–4 each center on one or two women's life histories. Among the first- and second-generation state workers, women were a small minority. The state hired women as "family dependent workers" in the 1950s and then as "collective workers" in the 1980s: both categorizations accommodated the need for labor exploitation while achieving an appearance of gender equality. Because forestry work units are urban enterprises located on rural land, there were many interactions and tensions between peasants and forestry workers. Stories from state workers, family dependent workers, collective workers, and peasants help paint the multifaceted picture of Chinese forestry.

Chapters 1 and 2 explore the accumulation of capital at the beginning of Chinese socialism. Tracing the stories of a first-generation state worker and two first-generation family dependent workers, these chapters demonstrate how the state took up and reinforced the gender and rural/urban divisions to enable the expropriation of land and timber and the mass mobilization of labor for the state forestry in the 1950s and 1960s—that is to say, the establishment of the socialist economic system in forestry.

Chapters 3 and 4 investigate the accumulation of capital during China's transition to state capitalism. Through the stories of a peasant and a second-generation collective worker, these two chapters show how the strategies used for capital accumulation under socialism, especially the exploitation of gender and rural/urban divisions, were inherited and applied under state capitalism. The women's narratives show their shifting feelings and understandings about their laboring past and the forestry economy and show how they applied different knowledge systems in their oppositional actions.

Chapter 5 shows how individual feelings of injustice grew into applied knowledge and skills to demand material and emotional recognition and to act collectively. The practice of "speaking bitterness" was a Maoist ideological educational tool that encouraged people without formal education, namely women and peasants, to give voice to grievances as a means of developing class consciousness. My grandmother (with whom the book begins) and other first-generation women workers learned to use the genre of speaking bitterness to narrate their feelings of grievance in their personal and public lives and to merge different knowledge systems. Speaking bitterness, in their individual and group actions, could either cater to the state or oppose it.

Chapter 6 examines a collective action that demonstrates the lag between women workers' experiences of exploitation and their knowledge development and oppositional actions. Because I participated in this action from its very beginning in 2014, my account captures in detail how the protesters processed different feelings of injustice and employed different forms of analytical knowledge about the nature of the Chinese economy at various stages of their activism.

The stories here illustrate what historian Gail Hershatter calls "the moments when the political is personal."[26] The Chinese state's revolutions, reforms, and capital accumulation manifested themselves in women's individual accounts of entanglements and feelings. The stories also reveal moments when the personal converges with the political, as when hundreds of women and men came together to petition the government nonstop for over a decade and to develop their own critical analysis of the Chinese state and economic development.

The workers' stories illustrate the accumulation of capital under both socialism and capitalism and how the amassed grievances and knowledge of individuals converged into collective resistance.

ONE

MIGRATION FOR WORK
IN FORESTRY

Zuo Xueyuan, born in 1963 and raised in a family of sawmill workers, was one of the former workers who watched with me as electric cutting torches dismantled a crane during the demolition of the Shaowu Sawmill in 2013. On one side of the street running through the mill had been the log and coal storage, railroad track, workshops, power plants with their towering chimneys, and other infrastructure for industrial production. On the other side stood facilities that fulfilled people's everyday needs, such as housing, canteens, a library, schools, a clinic, a day-care center, and small shops. Standing in the log yard, Zuo recalled that the "sawmill kids" often picked up wood chips here to fuel their stoves at home. Most Shaowu households used wood-burning stoves until the early 1990s. Although taking the wood was technically stealing, the managers at the mill tended to ignore it. When workers or their children took the wood home, they crossed the street that formed both a literal and a symbolic boundary between their work and their personal and family lives.

During the Maoist era the urban district of Shaowu consisted of only about six blocks. The sawmill stood just outside. Rezoned as urban land in the late 1970s, the area around the sawmill belonged to peasant villages in the 1960s and most of the 1970s. Zuo recalled: "We were really bad kids at that time and often bullied the village kids." The sawmill kids guarded their "territory" and chased off the peasant kids who tried to pick up wood chips for their own homes.

This childhood rivalry reflects the division between urban and rural in the Maoist era, fostered by the state and reinforced by the residents. For the workers, the sawmill was not only their workplace but also their home, so that even though they were relative newcomers, they felt a sense of ownership over the land and materials.

In the early years of forestry in Fujian, the late 1950s to the early 1960s, state-engineered migration provided a substantial labor force for forest farms and sawmills. New policies enabled the collectivization of forest ownership and a state monopoly over tree harvesting and commercialization. All these changes were informed by the state-created divide between rural and urban life, the background against which Zuo's childhood story unfolded.

Zuo Xueyuan's mother, Zhuang Jinxian, was one of the twenty thousand peasants who migrated from the northern province of Shandong to work in the Fujianese wood industry between 1958 and 1960. Zhuang, one of a small number of women recruited with the official status of state worker, was exceptional in that she became a cadre (a staff member tasked with the management of state or party affairs) in the sawmill and was later given the Model Laborer award. Her experience giving numerous award-winner's speeches at official conferences influenced the way she organized her life story, including how she talked about her roles as a daughter, wife, and mother as well as her contribution to socialist development.[1]

The stories of forestry workers like Zhuang illustrate how the physical and ideological features of the forestry units shaped workers' lives and their interactions with the villagers who lived nearby.

Transplanting Laborers

Zhuang Jinxian was born in a village in Cao County of southwestern Shandong in 1939, when northern China was under Japanese colonial control. To escape the ravages of war, her family fled when she was a small child, first to other villages and then to a city nearby for more employment opportunities. Zhuang's mother worked as a cook. Whenever the employer gave out scraps of leftover food, she saved them to feed her children. Once, when the employer found two pieces of dried sweet potato her mother had pocketed, he called her a thief. Her mother cried, explaining, "I'd rather die than steal. These are what you gave me earlier. I didn't eat them. I was saving them for my kids." Despite her mother's work, the family often didn't have enough food. Begging in the street as a child, Zhuang was once bitten by a dog.

On taking control of northern China in 1949, the Communist Party sent refugees back to their home villages to reduce the unemployed and homeless urban population and rebuild the urban economy.[2] Zhuang's family was among them. During the 1950s, starting with the Land Reform Movement, changes in land, labor, and material redistribution policies tremendously widened the rural/urban divide. Rural residents obtained collective land tenure. On returning to their home village, the Zhuangs were allocated a small piece of land from the rural collective for their subsistence.

Believing that peasants could and should be self-sufficient, the central government effectively tied them to the land, offering few resources or services. In 1958, a new household registration system legally categorized rural residents in the countryside as an "agricultural population" (*nongye renkou*), restricted to working in agriculture. Meanwhile, urban residents, stripped of land ownership, were placed under the "urban public goods regime."[3] They were assigned secure jobs as part of a package of entitlements that included food, subsidized housing, consumer goods, education, and medical care. Industrial factories were overwhelmingly located in cities and nearly banned in the countryside, with the exception of industries that directly served agriculture and mining.

Rural and urban populations were not only divided but also placed in an unequal relation. The state set agricultural product prices lower than those of goods manufactured in urban factories. Villagers were required to meet grain-production quotas to supply the urban population before they could obtain grain for themselves. Both measures ensured the state's ability to expropriate agricultural products for urban industrialization.[4] Beyond ensuring that the urban population was fed, these "price scissors" and the state monopoly over the food supply enabled the state to impose low wages for the urban workers so as to decrease the costs of industrial production and accumulate extra capital for industrialization. Under the price scissors and grain production quota, Zhuang's village and many nearby villages suffered severe scarcities of food. Some peasants breached the urban/rural divide and fled to the cities again.

Besides the food shortage, what Zhuang remembered most clearly about living in the village in the 1950s was her round-the-clock work at home and the excitement of participating in the Communist campaigns.

In 1954, when she was fifteen, Zhuang attended almost a year of night school. Because most village women were illiterate at that time, Zhuang considered herself very fortunate to be able to attend school. She knew that she would not be able to stay for long. As the eldest child, she soon dropped out to work in the household textile workshop and to take care of her four younger brothers. When recalling how she had to carry the baby all day while doing textile work (for example, spinning) and house chores like cooking, Zhuang showed me her left hand, which was permanently deformed, with the index finger and middle finger both bent toward the ring finger. She told me that this was a result of having her hand in an excessively flexed position for long periods carrying or holding a baby.

Around the time she dropped out of school, Zhuang joined the Communist Youth League of China and became active in political campaigns. In 1958, she started working as a bookkeeper at a rural credit cooperative and studying a dictionary to increase her vocabulary.

That year, Mao Zedong launched the Great Leap Forward, a national campaign aiming to dramatically accelerate economic development. Production units were amalgamated into large communes that also functioned as government structures. Under the coordination of the commune, many rural men worked for weeks on ambitious infrastructure projects in irrigation and road building far from their home villages. Men were also organized to work at furnaces smelting steel in an effort to decentralize and expand industrial production. As a result, villages suffered a severe agricultural labor shortage. Women were mobilized to do fieldwork on the collective farms and sometimes to join in the infrastructure work and small-scale iron and steel production.[5] As a state-endorsed campaign activist who was passionate about the socialist vision, Zhuang remembered this period as "great fun," associated with the excitement of "liberating" others and creating a better collective future.

I was already a village committee member when the Great Leap Forward started in 1958. I donated every steel object from my home [to the steelworks], including our washbasin. My mother was mad at me, but I told her that I needed to take the lead. I donated our food from home as well. It was a wild time!

As a leader of the village Women's Federation, my responsibility was to mobilize women to work on the collective farm. Most women did cooking and other domestic chores at that time, and we wanted to organize them to go out and work. We brought them out to carry sand, which was great fun. To mobilize them, we visited their homes to call on them one by one. Some of them or their families did not agree. We just cut their hair, the women's braids. It was so crazy! Some of them didn't want their braids to be cut, but we didn't do too much talking. Having the braids cut off means going out to work. To emancipate women, women must go out to work, so men and women can be equal.

However, like most rural women at that time, Zhuang Jinxian also suffered from exhaustion and health problems. This was partly because the local leaders, including women cadres like herself, prioritized production over women's needs.

The collapse of the Great Leap in 1959 led to a catastrophic famine between 1959 and 1961. Because the state's grain monopoly had divided urban and rural residents into consumers and producers of grain, and privileged cities over villages, the peasants, including those in Zhuang's village, faced starvation.[6] Amidst all this suffering, Zhuang and her new husband learned of a chance of working in Fujian.

In 1960, the Shandong provincial government was recruiting peasants from the populous western inland region to establish a state forestry in the southeastern frontier region of Fujian. Expanding military capacity and industrial development in Fujian was crucial to China's plan to outrival Taiwan. Forestry, as well as the iron and steel industry, was developed in the inland part of Fujian to avoid direct attack from Taiwan. The country's railroad construction capacity was limited not by a lack of iron and steel, as is often supposed, but by a shortage of timber suitable for the manufacture of railroad ties.[7] The government was also eager to produce timber for constructing mine shafts. It aimed to recruit twenty thousand people to work in Fujian for two years, using the rhetoric that since Shandong was populous but without much forestry, and Fujian lacked the labor power necessary for its forestry development, an exchange of labor and human resources would be mutually beneficial.

This mass-migration model had plenty of precedent. Interprovincial migration had become a common strategy by which the Chinese state mobilized cheaper labor to build industries or to maintain farms and mines providing resources directly to factories. Migration programs often moved tens of thousands of people from the inner Chinese provinces to rubber plantations and specialty timber forests in the southwestern provinces of Yunnan, Guangxi, and Guizhou. Most of the enlistees for the Qinghai and Xinjiang Construction Corps, located in the northwest, came from rural lands over one thousand miles away.[8] In total, tens of millions migrated from their rural homelands between the mid-1950s and the 1960s.

Migration was not new. Many Chinese in the nineteenth and early twentieth centuries had fled war, poverty, and famine. What differentiated the population resettlements of the 1950s and 1960s was the central socialist planning that drove them. The grain-rationing system, together with the household registration system, effectively divided the Chinese population into rural grain producers and urban grain consumers. In agricultural production, the grain consumption of urban residents was prioritized, and urban households were issued coupons for their rations of grain. Rural residents could not access the urban grain-coupon system to obtain food. These measures prevented residents from relocating at will. National and provincial governments, on the other hand, were able to coordinate the transfer of people between rural and urban areas as well as across provinces. In the Mao era, the state was the central actor in mobilizing human resources for economic development.

The question of how much choice migrants like Zhuang and her husband had in deciding to move is difficult to answer. The responses from workers I interviewed were greatly conditioned by their current situations. While the majority talked about their migration unemotionally, as a neutral fact, the first-generation forest farm workers used phrases such as "The state lied to us." These workers had spent a decade, from 1998 to 2008, protesting the Shaowu city government's nonpayment of their pensions before I interviewed them. Their collective activism, in which they emphasized the state's manipulation of labor migration as a justification for compensation, had a big impact on their daily narrative and their retrospective view of the migration program.

It is also a question to which these migrants had no clear-cut answer. Although they were nominally volunteers, the state controlled their food and employment arrangements. For rural dwellers with long experience of poverty, hunger, and exhaustion, migration represented a chance to elevate their status from peasant to state-enterprise worker and improve their living conditions. Many were selected to join these programs because of their loyalty to the Communist Party. For these people, the move was about survival, appreciation, and political conviction.

All of these motivations applied to Zhuang Jinxian. She "felt fortunate to be selected." The recruiters promised food for the peasants who migrated and extra income that they could send back home. As the oldest child, Zhuang had grown up with the responsibility of caring for other family members. Now that she was married, she and her husband had two families dependent on their financial help. Although she was frightened by rumors that the Fujian mountains were full of snakes, she knew her family needed that income to survive.

At the same time, Zhuang felt proud to be among the small number of women recruited to a project that was significant for the state and socialist development. The selection criteria for these new official state workers specified either some formal education or membership in the Communist Party or Youth League. That ruled out most rural women because they were illiterate. Zhuang was an exception because she had attended night school for a year. She was also active in the Communist campaigns.

Being uprooted from their home villages in the northern plain and transplanted to southern mountains 1,500 kilometers away was a great challenge for Zhuang Jinxian and all the other migrants. She and her husband both initially worked at Dragon Lake Forest Farm, one of the thirteen farms in Shaowu. Zhuang was assigned what she considered a plum job as a bookkeeper, since she had similar experience from her Shandong village. Because the farm was just starting up, all workers had many additional duties. Zhuang was often asked to clear underbrush and grass before and after logging operations, a much more physically demanding job than her office work.

Zhuang's husband worked as a logger, which was especially dangerous and difficult for northerners who had grown up on the plains and were not used to climbing hills or dealing with the local flora and fauna. Because no machinery was available in the first few years, the crews skidded the small logs downhill and used a temporary wooden system called a donkey to move larger logs. To make a donkey, the loggers laid some smaller logs on the ground that functioned as rollers for moving larger logs by hand. After that, a more advanced system was introduced, which involved wooden tracks and carts and pulling ropes by hand. In the late 1960s, a more permanent, manually operated metal cable system came into use.

As the recruiters had promised, the food supply was reliable, although choices were limited. The workers ate rice steamed in bamboo tubes, pickled fish, and vegetables every day. Because they were building the farm from scratch, the housing was crude: sheds made of grass, mud, and bamboo strips. The roofs leaked whenever it rained. Zhuang's first two children were born in her room on the farm with the assistance of the village midwife. She had heard that some other forest farms ordered workers to send their kids home to their grandparents, but her supervisor allowed her to keep an eye on them while she worked.

In 1962, two years after Zhuang and her husband and the others arrived on the farm, and right around the time they thought they would return to Shandong, they were ordered to stay for good. Government control ensured compliance; only a few workers were able to flee back home. Around the same time, over a hundred male peasants from Zhejiang and about sixty urban residents from Shanghai joined the Dragon Lake Forest Farm. Compared to Shandong, Shanghai and Zhejiang are both much closer to Fujian. Zhejiang is just north of Fujian, and Shanghai is just north of Zhejiang. The Shanghai workers were all single, including twenty-two women aged seventeen to nineteen who had been educated through middle school—a luxury at the time. They were the only unmarried women on the farm. Some women also came from Shandong, but they were all married and came with their husbands. Recalling their reasons for joining the migration, these Shanghai women talked about their desire "to leave home to have adventures" after hearing about their peers' participation in other programs bolstering Chinese industry and agriculture.

These young Shanghai women came with cheerful and playful spirits. They found the twenty hours of train and boat travel from the city a lot of fun, praised the azalea flowers that covered the mountains in spring, and enjoyed mixing steamed rice with the lard they had brought from Shanghai. Like Zhuang when starting her career as a leader of the Shandong village's Women's Federation in 1958, they were young, single, outspoken, and ready to embrace the adventure of collective life. However, they were perhaps not ready for the backbreaking manual labor. They also loudly and constantly complained about the poor living conditions on the farm.

Most of these women ended up marrying non-Shanghai workers. On the farm, a man who knew how to get food was more attractive than one who had a formal education. Shanghainese men hardly knew how to take care of themselves in the mountainous countryside, but the workers from Shandong and Zhejiang, who mostly had rural origins, knew how to plant vegetables and catch freshwater snails and fish. Courtship was not complicated on the farm: if a woman liked a man, she offered to help wash his clothes, and they spent more time together away from others. To get married, a couple simply shoved two wooden-board beds together to make a double bed and gave brown-sugar candy to their coworkers. The farm gave each married couple a separate room, and the chance to move out of the makeshift dormitory was the primary reason why the single workers all rapidly married.

Expropriating Forests

China in the 1950s witnessed several state dispossessions of rural land, resources, and labor. The state confiscated land from landlords and rich peasants to establish rural collectives. The rural/urban segregation and the grain-rationing system enabled the state to deprive the peasants of their entitlement to their agricultural products and to expropriate their labor for interprovincial industrialization projects. These policies set up the structure for later labor exploitation and were a crucial component of socialist Chinese capital accumulation. The state forestry was a part of this project.

The development of the state wood industry also required timber, ideally at a low cost. The process of turning forests into raw materials for the state enterprises' production was neither swift nor smooth. It started with a decade-long series of frequent policy shifts, leading to both intentional and unintentional changes in the peasants' relationship with the forests. These policies also initiated decades of friction between the state forest farms and the villages. Within the first fifteen years of the founding of the People's Republic of China, ownership of the forests in southern China was shifted no fewer than ten times, whether between peasant households or to different levels of village cooperatives.

The organization of the labor force changed with the different forms of ownership (see table 1.1). From 1951 to 1954, workers were organized into mutual-aid teams. These involved temporary sharing of labor and some capital; individual households remained the basic unit of ownership and production.

In 1954, mutual-aid teams were phased out in favor of cooperatives, in which tools and labor were shared on a permanent basis. In elementary cooperatives (1954–56), members retained ownership of their land but earned income based on their shares of the land. Advanced cooperatives (1955–1957) collectively owned most of the land and distributed farm profits to members mainly according to their labor contributions. The average advanced cooperative was made up of 170 families and more than seven hundred people.

From 1958 to the early 1980s, labor was organized into large people's communes, with an average of 5,400 households and twenty thousand to thirty thousand individual members. The communes had governmental, political, and economic functions. They were subdivided into production brigades (roughly equal to townships or big villages after the mid-1980s) and further into production teams (roughly equal to small villages).

As a result of these frequent upheavals, the villagers, as individuals and groups, lost faith that their rights would be honored and therefore abdicated any interest in managing the forests. Furthermore, although the Fujianese villages collectively owned forests in the mid- and late 1950s, the socialist planned economy did not give them the legal right to commodify timber, which the central government considered a crucial resource for industri-

Changing Forest Tenure Policy, 1644–1979

1644–1949	Individual landlords owned forestland in the mountains but mostly lived far away and left forests to be managed in which peasant tenants.
1950–52	Land Reform Campaign distributed land, forests, and other means of production equally to farming households.
1953–55	Agricultural production was organized at three levels: households, mutual aid teams, and elementary cooperatives.
1956	96 percent of rural households were incorporated into advanced cooperatives; land, forests, and other means of production were transferred from individual households to advanced cooperatives.
1958	Forests were transferred from advanced cooperatives to people's communes.
1959–61	Agricultural failure and famine.
1961–64	Forest ownership and management devolved from communes to production teams or production brigades: nontimber forests were reallocated to nearby households.
1966–79	Scattered areas of nontimber trees owned by households were collectivized.

Source: Liu Dachang, "Tenure and Management of Non-State Forests in China since 1950: A Historical Review," *Environmental History* 6, no. 2 (2001): 239–63.

alization (along with concrete and steel). The state monopolized timber production, transportation, and trade. The villagers could use wood only for limited household needs, including fuel and building homes. This legal change facilitated expropriation of the timber for the state's industrial production and capital accumulation.

When the state forest farms were established in Shaowu in 1958, the city government coordinated a lease in which the villages were required to loan half of their forests to the forest farms. The farms had rights to fell, sell, and plant trees, while paying the villages annual rents. The leases did not specify a tenure, so the deal was understood by the camp authorities and the villagers as potentially permanent. All harvested logs were sent to the Shaowu State Sawmill for processing, sale, and transportation.

The villagers were unhappy about being stripped of a significant part of their rights to the trees, but they lacked power to bargain with the state, and they had lost motivation after years of constantly shifting ownership. Besides, they had enough timber for their household needs.[9] Still, "everyday forms of resistance" by the disadvantaged peasants never stopped.[10] The peasants often stole trees and branches from the forest farm. Mischievous village kids even stole the vegetables the workers grew in the fields around the farms.

Zhuang Jinxian remembered the small frictions between the forest farm workers and the peasants as annoying, but not serious. The workers avoided direct conflict with the villagers. They realized that the peasants, who had lived there for generations, knew the mountains so well that they could easily disrupt production or conduct illegal logging if they wanted to. There were no fences between the forests leased to the forest farms and those still managed by the villagers. State power, no matter how strong, could not enable the farm workers to patrol entire mountains. They knew it would be wise to play fair with the villagers. They paved the roads around the farms and the villages, which eased travel for the villagers and went a long way toward keeping the peace.

Work and Life in State Forestry

Daily trucks from the thirteen forest farms delivered timber along the newly paved roads to the Shaowu Sawmill, also built in 1958. Originally meant to process, temporarily store, and then ship logs, the mill faced many challenges. The workers' sheds, built from bamboo and grass, burned down in 1959 and again in 1960. When leveling a field for storing logs, the workers unearthed many human bones and shackles. Had it once been an execution ground? The workers were scared because disturbing human remains—and therefore the afterlives of those who had died—could bring bad fortune or even a curse.

In the early 1960s, the sawmill began producing railroad ties from timber heartwood and packing materials from the softer outside layers of the logs.

In 1966, they started two more workshops to produce plywood (manufactured by gluing together thin layers of wood) and particleboard (made from wood chips, sawmill shavings, and other waste materials heated, glued, and compressed), using waste products and materials rejected from railroad tie production. Particleboard was an alternative to plywood when timber was in short supply. At that time, the sawmill prioritized production of ties, packing boards, plywood, and particleboard, in that order.

With the establishment of these two workshops, Zhuang Jinxian and her husband were transferred from arduous forest farm work to slightly easier jobs at the mill. But the move meant they had to send their small children away.

> Looking at our kids, the construction manager, a Shanghainese man wearing pointed leather shoes, demanded: "How can you go to training like this? It's not okay. Deal with the kids right now." It was not negotiable. I first took the kids back to Shandong. My son was three, and my daughter was turning one. We stayed at my hometown for less than three days, and my mother rejected my request for help, because my family was too poor to take care of two more people. I had to take them back to a Fujianese village, where I hired a local peasant as a nanny. A woman from Shandong whom I had known before was living in the same village and agreed to monitor the nannying.

When it was time for Zhuang to leave, the nanny took the kids to see their mother off.

> My daughter was still breastfeeding. On the way from the nanny's home to the train station, I had stopped giving her breast milk. She cried so hard that she lost her voice. I was sitting in the train and looking through the window, and my kids were out there crying. But I had to leave. The day after I came back to Shaowu, we took off to Shanghai and trained in a sawmill there for over half a year. Afterwards, the production of the two new workshops started. My husband worked on the plywood workshop, and I worked on the particleboard one.

When Zhuang went to pick up her children a year later, she was sad to find that they didn't recognize her. When her third and last child was born in 1970, Zhuang was legally entitled to fifty-six days of maternity leave, but she took only forty days off. A new machine was being installed, and she did not want to miss the training. The sawmill had started a day-care center, but Zhuang's infant daughter was still on the waiting list. She asked her older children, ages seven and five, to babysit their little sister. Too young to take care of the baby very well, once they scalded her foot with hot water. After that, Zhuang decided to take the baby to work, as many other families with young children did. Since workers were assigned to tasks in pairs, they managed to take turns working and watching one another's children.

> I put [my baby daughter] on a particleboard in the workshop. I was not really watching her, but there were many other workers who dropped by from time to time to hold her or play with her. She was such a cute and playful baby. It was quite hot in the workshop, so her bottom was always red. . . .
>
> She finally got into the day-care center. Besides the long break around noon, we had two breastfeeding breaks: each was thirty minutes long, one in the morning, the other in the afternoon. I always ran to the day care during the breastfeeding breaks. She was so hungry, and I had too much milk, so she constantly threw up after nursing. Ah, now I recall, that time was too painful. There was only half an hour. She threw up all the milk, but I had to return to work. Even the daycare helper told me, "You can't always rush like this. It's too intense." I was a diligent worker, and I did not want to be late to my work. We worked in three eight-hour shifts and were unable to eat at regular hours. I never complained about my work. When the machine was broken, I manually pushed the board in. I didn't care about money and rewards.

The Shaowu State Sawmill, a *danwei* (work unit), was a cradle-to-grave organization.[11] In the 1960s and 1970s, it included employee housing, canteens, public showers, clinics, an auditorium, an activity center, a farmers' market, convenience stores, a day-care center, and schools. Sawmill workers also constructed and maintained utilities to serve the mill, including an electrical power station and lines, telephone lines, water towers, and water and sewage pipes. The mill provided workers and their families with medical care, paid maternity leave, disability pensions, retirement pensions, funeral benefits, and financial support for the families of workers killed in the workplace.

The design of the *danwei* was influenced by the Soviet socialist ideal of creating a communal living environment that combined everyday life and collective labor to increase productivity and forge proletarian social relationships and collective consciousness.[12] Just as traditional Confucian households built a wall around the houses of an extended family, a typical *danwei* encompassed workplace, residences, and social facilities.[13] The three biggest work units in urban Shaowu from the 1960s to the 1980s were the sawmill, a paper mill, and a textile mill. Each had roughly one thousand to three thousand dwellers: the workers and their families.

Although residents occasionally formed networks based on their places of origin, lineage ties, and ethnicities, the *danwei* was the primary unit of community building.[14] The most commonly asked question of a stranger at that period was "Which *danwei* are you from?" Even when the question was abbreviated to "Where are you from?," the answer would include that person's *danwei*. Anyone asking your *danwei* would learn your identity, status, and networks, as well as how they should treat you. People in a *danwei* were generally better provided with food, clothing, and household amenities than the minority of urban people who were not in one, though the level of support varied.[15] Only a wall separated the Shaowu Sawmill and the Shaowu Paper Mill, but people kept to their own mill, and the sawmill residents saw themselves as superior to the paper mill people, because the sawmill was much better funded and considered a higher-status *danwei*.

Danwei were also the local vehicles for the state's political campaigns and ideological education. The cadres not only functioned as managers overseeing workers and implementing state policies during campaigns but also exemplified a sort of socialist morality within the *danwei* in their everyday life.

Zhuang was promoted to be the particleboard workshop supervisor in the early 1970s. Among the five thousand people who had worked at the sawmill since its creation, there were only four women cadres. In addition to her Model Laborer award, she was granted an Award for Excellent Thought Work (a recognition of her accomplishments in political education) from the city and the prefecture, and she was widely respected by the sawmill

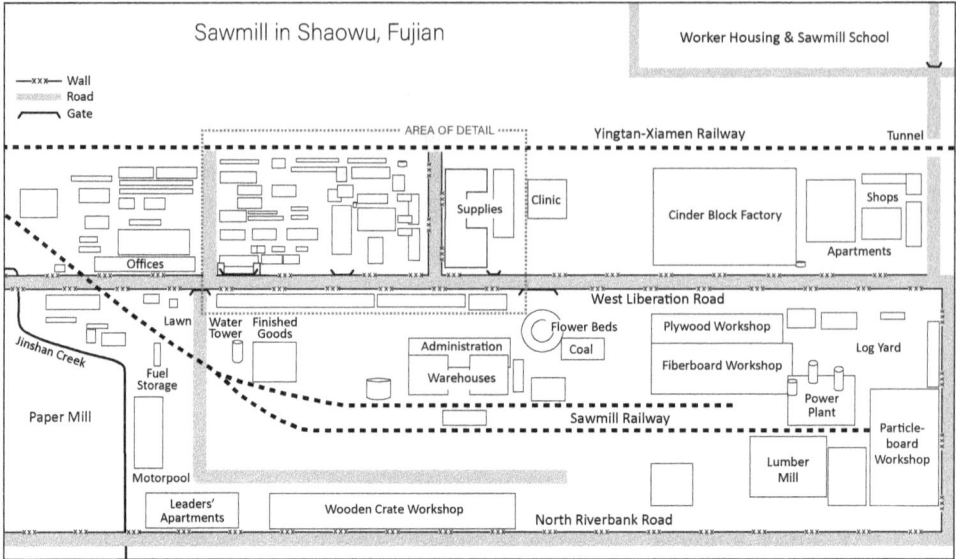

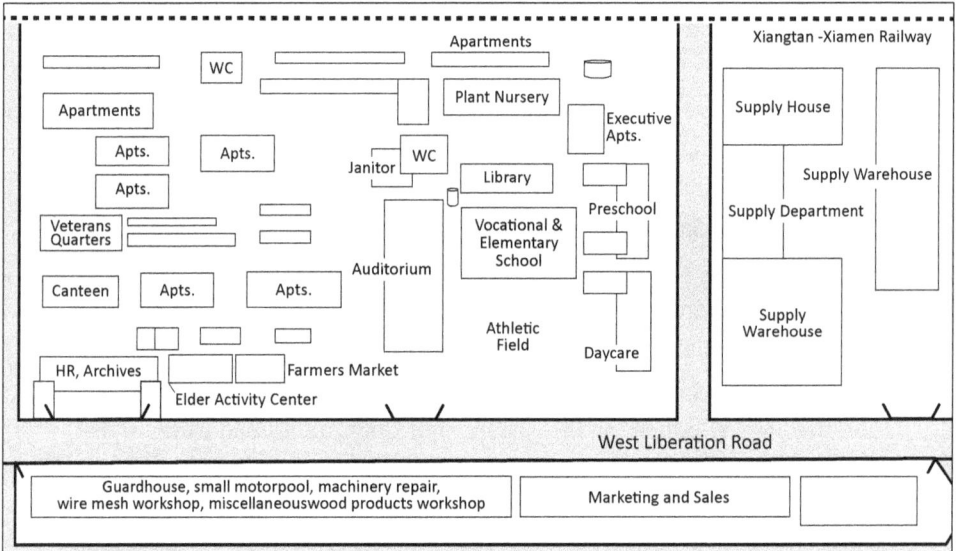

Map of Shaowu Sawmill in the 1980s. Original Chinese map by Shaoping Zhou and Shuxuan Zhou, with label translation assistance from Stevan Harrell. Cartography by Lily Crandall-Oral.

workers and their families. Zhuang always distributed her award bonuses to the workers in her workshop, and in narrating her life story to me she emphasized that she had never abused her power in order to seek jobs for her children. The cadres were supposed to demonstrate their socialist political consciousness by advancing equity and preventing corruption. Redistributing resources fairly demonstrated their ideological commitment.

Workshop cadres like Zhuang could preapprove household registration for new workers (and occasionally their family members), approve travel and time off from work, authorize the reimbursement of special medical costs, and intervene in how the courts and police treated the workers they supervised.[16] The sociologist Andrew Walder, in one of the first books describing the internal political mechanism of the *danwei*, observed that *danwei* cadres had so much power that their treatment of workers often mixed public and private considerations. A cadre might assign a job to the worker they thought was best qualified, which resulted in a better relationship with this worker and long-term loyalty toward the cadre. Or they might select a worker with whom they had a good relationship, who would then work hard in order to show loyalty to the cadre. The internal economic and political mechanisms of the *danwei* made workers and cadres mutually dependent.

Sawmill workers often said: "Each *danwei* is a small society." Through the *danwei* and the cadres, the state managed social reproduction as well as industrial production. The responsibilities of a cadre like Zhuang Jinxian even included mediating workers' personal conflicts.

> Workers from different areas of the country—Shandong, Fujian, and Shanghai and Zhejiang—were likely to have disagreements. I tried to befriend everyone and have heart-to-heart talks with them, no matter where they were from, and even if some of them made fun of me behind my back. Whoever had difficulties, I went to help them. Uniting the workers was crucial for production.
>
> Wugui [Turtle], a worker in my mill—his wife looked down on him, and they fought every day. I was worried that would affect his work, so I went to his home and talked with his wife. We talked about all the small everyday issues in the household, and I asked her if there was anything I could help with.

She later reassigned Turtle to a better job. "They didn't divorce, and he is still very grateful to me. I successfully prevented many married couples from divorcing. As long as we cadres tried very hard to empathize with the workers, caring for them heart to heart, . . . we could do well in thought work."

Zhuang's words reveal the challenges of managing the sawmill labor force. Workers from different regions formed cliques and were often hostile to others. Meanwhile, the workers' families had internal conflicts, like all families, but when entire extended families all worked in the same mill, the conflicts sometimes spilled onto the shop floor. For the sake of production, and to prevent industrial unrest, all these conflicts needed to be managed.

Zhuang Jinxian's attention to the workers' lives and her efforts to prevent manufacturing disruptions by anticipating and deescalating conflicts were essential to the smooth functioning of the mill. In turn, the workers and their families actively requested that the cadres help solve their problems. Parents might ask a cadre to find a job for a child coming of age. If a worker developed a mental or physical disability, it was the cadre who would request the worker's transfer to a more suitable position or the payment of a pension.

For Zhuang Jinxian, moving from the Dragon Lake Forest Farm to the Shaowu Sawmill had been a bit of luck. She escaped backbreaking work and a tough living environment. She was surprised when the Dragon Lake Forest Farm was later transformed into a model *danwei*, where she and other sawmill workers were often sent to observe operations beginning in the late 1970s. Rapid state-funded construction had turned it into a modern place.

The forest farm headquarters and its four satellite working and living areas were concrete enclosures spread across several mountainsides, miles apart. The modern brick and concrete structures separated the *danwei* from their rural surroundings. The village houses were mostly built with mud, mud bricks, and bamboo strips, and their roads remained unpaved through the end of the twentieth century. When I visited the farm in 2014 and 2018, many buildings still stood, though most had been abandoned. Decades of spring and summer rains had painted black streaks of mold down the white exterior walls. The dark red and green paint on the wooden windows had weathered surprisingly well. The outdoor basketball court had been quiet

Dragon Lake Forest Farm, 2014. *Top*: Dragon Lake Forest Farm: apartments and basketball court; *bottom*: office building with a cafeteria on the ground floor.

since 2000, but the slogan "Enhancing People's Body Quality," painted in red, remained just legible. Three loudspeakers were still mounted atop the building in the center of the farm, silent reminders of the music, news, and announcements they had once played.

The farm's infrastructure, built from scratch, was separate from that of the neighboring village. The peasants were banned from using the work unit's facilities, and their village had no modern infrastructure. The villagers finally started using a hydroelectric generator installed in a nearby river in the late 1980s.[17]

The forest farm workers also received more rationed goods than the villagers and even the sawmill workers. After 1955, cooking oil, cotton cloth, and other necessities began to be rationed in the same way as grain. When she returned to the farm, Zhuang was surprised to learn that it had a higher standard of living than the sawmill.

People growing up in the Dragon Lake Village between the 1960s and the 1980s recalled that they had always envied the farm workers: "They had much more food than we did. They received rice and oil every month. We villagers didn't have much to eat in those years, not like them. They even often had meat to eat. Every lunch and dinner time, seeing the smoke rising from the forest farm, we envied them a lot." At the same time, they found the workers annoying: "Those northern migrants who came to our place were so arrogant that they looked down on us." People who worked or grew up in the Dragon Lake Forest Farm tell the story from the other side: "Our forest farm was a state-owned enterprise *danwei*! The villages were very dirty, unorganized, and backward, while our unit was tidy and orderly."

Most scholarly and popular books portray a sharp division between rural and urban in the Mao era: the rural population lived on rural land, performed agricultural labor, and was managed through village collectives, while the urban population lived in cities, worked in factories, and was managed through work units. But among state forest farms and workers during that period, that distinction was blurred. Even though the forest farms were located in the countryside and surrounded by rural villages, the state-owned land, the types of buildings and infrastructure, and the *danwei* system identified them as urban. The state workers even held urban (nonagricultural) household registrations.

Other state farms and mines also had urban *danwei* administrations yet were located on rural land.[18] Meanwhile, as the result of massive interprovincial labor migration, much larger operations, such as the Xinjiang and Qinghai Construction Corps, the Great Northern Wilderness Development, and the Third Front Construction, transformed rural land into urban land and continued to produce agricultural and industrial materials for the state economy. These entities' ambiguous rural-urban status raises other questions: What are the implications of having urban industries on rural land? How did it affect people's lives and ideas?

First and foremost, these cross-sectoral enterprises not only provided low-cost means of production and producers to the state economy but also reinforced the ideological differences between urban and rural, industry and agriculture, workers and peasants.

The placement of a *danwei* in a rural area underscored the notion that socialism could transform everything. This urban place in rural space juxtaposed the "advancement" of urban industrialization with the "backwardness" of rural agriculture, bolstering the argument that urbanization was the only path to socialist modernization. State workers exemplified labor subjects representing a socialist modernity and were thus legitimized as the force selected to work on the rural and natural landscape of the forests, whereas peasants were excluded from the modernization program on their native land. Even more ironically, these state workers had been peasants themselves before their migration.

The state workers were still underpaid. They received better welfare and benefits than their rural counterparts, but only because the latter experienced constant expropriation of the products of their labor.[19] Because the state monopolized the food supply and provided the workers with cheap grain and land that they expropriated from the villages, the state could limit the state workers' compensation and keep labor costs low. China's urban/rural divide and the state forestry's in-between spatial and administrative status made possible the establishment of state wood production and capital accumulation.

Trade in Humans and Trees

When the northern peasants migrated to mountainous southern China, both the natural environment and the working environment were unfamiliar. Their very bodies were transplanted to serve the Chinese socialist state's ambitions for modernization and development. The local feng shui master interpreted the deadly workplace accidents of the Dragon Lake Forest Farm workers in the 1960s as nature's way of punishing the force that was harming it. That same force was uprooting the workers from their homes to carry out those harms. This interpretation could serve as a metaphor for the way that forestry production consumed both laborers and natural resources for industrialization and capital accumulation. Laborers and natural resources stood in parallel positions within this industry. The workers described the nature of the new state forestry in their own way: "Shandong gave Fujian people, and Fujian gave Shandong wood." In the eyes of the state, both people and trees were raw materials for the project of developing the socialist nation.

However, this process was not simply an equal exchange between two provincial economies. In purely economic terms, it began with the expropriation of both migrant labor and the means of production (trees and land). This created use value in the form of timber, which was sold at an exchange value determined by the state monopoly. The buyers (usually state enterprises or government agencies) used timber as raw material in projects that created more value for the state. Throughout this process, the state, as the only coordinator in the markets of labor, resources, and goods, extracted all surplus value. The state thus acted as the representative of capital. It was the amalgamation of massive amounts of labor along with vast natural resources—the combination of expropriation and exploitation, coordinated by the state—that drove capital accumulation.

In his analysis of Chinese socialism, Wen Tiejun, a renowned scholar of political economy and rural issues, argues that China, unable to plunder foreign resources through colonialism in the Western manner, instead accumulated primary capital from internal agricultural surpluses during the Maoist era. He details how China expropriated the rural surplus to the urban sphere for industrialization through the commune system, state-controlled purchasing and marketing, the household registration system, and the rationing of food and material goods.[20] State forestry, Mao style, would not have been possible without these institutions.

Moving laborers from 1,500 kilometers away, instead of simply recruiting some of the local rural population as state workers, was advantageous to the state's capital accumulation operation. First, outsiders had no existing relationship with or knowledge about local land, forests, and ecosystems. They simply followed the state's directions on harvesting and planting trees. In fact, after living in Fujian forests for decades, most of the Shandong workers still couldn't identify many trees and plants in local ecosystems. The workers were taught to recognize three kinds of trees in Fujian forests: *song mu* (Chinese red pine, *Pinus tabuliformis*), *shan mu* (China fir, *Cunninghamia*), and *zhu zi* (bamboo). The rest, *za mu* (miscellaneous trees), were considered insignificant and could be used for firewood. Local peasants, whose families had developed sophisticated beliefs about how to work with the land, would not have been receptive to these simplistic guidelines.

Second, the lack of existing relationships between the Shandong migrants and Fujian locals made it possible to isolate the work units from the villages. Third, after being moved 1,500 kilometers away, Shandong workers, like Zhuang and her husband, would have found it hard to flee back to their home villages.

Stealing, expropriating, and exploiting outside labor to suppress a native population's control over land and resources is not unique. We have seen it happen in the long history of colonialism and imperialism worldwide. Migration removed some of the complicated human elements from the labor force, including attachment to natural surroundings—trees, land, animals—and to neighboring humans. This kind of detachment was crucial to the establishment of the Chinese state forestry.

TWO

THE DEPENDENTS

I sat in the courtyard of an apartment complex in Shaowu in spring 2014, watching elderly residents emerge from their homes after lunch. They chatted, played cards, or rested. An older man held the brown root of a plant, and with a curved blade, he removed the shoots, peeled it, and chopped it while a few others watched. Curious, I asked a *nainai* (grandmother) what it was and what the man was doing with it. She answered, "It's a medicinal plant, and I don't know its specific name and function. Only people who are from Zhejiang and Fujian, in the south, know. They often search for some medicinal plants in the woods and sell them. I came from Shandong, and we northerners don't recognize many special local plants." Another *nainai* jumped in: "When we first came here, we dependent workers (*jiashu gong*) were often hurt by the local living things. Didn't we have to go out there and pull out weeds, trim grass, and pick branches? We didn't know much about local fauna, and many times we directly hit hornets' nests. Lots of people got stung, some people's tongues were swollen, and a few even died from that. Some ate the wrong mushrooms and got poisoned, or touched the wrong plants and got a long-lasting allergic reaction."

In 1956, Mao Zedong decreed: "Humanity is destined to conquer nature." Accordingly, the state sent workers from the northern plain to transform the rural and natural landscape in the southern mountains. While this labor force—usually masculine in the dominant discourse—might sound sweeping, aggressive, and destructive to the original vegetation, the transformation hinged on another labor force that was more constructive and caring. These laborers reconditioned the land for cultivation and planted new trees, changing the species composition of the forest.[1] This entirely female workforce was registered as "family dependent workers."[2]

These paradoxically named dependent workers played important and often unappreciated roles in urban industrial enterprises. On the one hand, following the official rhetoric that "women hold up half the sky," national policies in the 1950s and 1960s promoted women's paid employment. On the other hand, gender inequalities in employment status and benefits were considerable. The life stories of two dependent workers, Xiaomei at the Dragon Lake Forest Farm and Laoniang at the Shaowu Sawmill, demonstrate how gender differences manifested in migration, work arrangements, and benefits allocation in the state wood industry. In their industrial jobs, the dependents were assigned ostensibly "lighter" and thus lower-paid tasks, but their narratives reveal that they actually carried out the most arduous and physically demanding duties. Meanwhile, because of the mostly inadequate supply of food and other goods (which did not increase proportionally with the addition of women and children to the household) and the absence of domestic support such as childcare benefits, these women had to perform domestic work at home as well as agricultural and animal-husbandry labor for the households and the work units. The multiple shifts that these dependent workers had to juggle were the means by which the state extracted surplus labor from these women.[3]

State Discourses about Women's Work

"Women hold up half the sky" was not empty talk in Maoist China. Both urban and rural women were swept into the paid labor market, new laws outlawed arranged marriage and child brides, and schools became coeducational. Women participated in the people's communes and urban industrialization, and there were some influential female labor models and cadres, including Zhuang Xinjian. Yet gender inequalities persisted.[4] For example, when Chinese villages were ordered to encourage housewives to work outside the home, most rural cooperatives and mutual aid teams used women as seasonal and on-demand labor, assigning them "lighter" jobs worth fewer work points.[5] In other words, women workers had lower status. Moreover, in rural areas, only agricultural work counted as production. Productive activities mostly done by women, such as handicrafts, were considered "backward" and earned no work points.[6] The state and the local production teams saw what women did at home as merely "help," rather than work.[7] In short, despite the Chinese state's efforts to remove the discourse of women's supposed inferiority and rectify women's oppression within the patriarchal family, it overlooked certain material practices that preserved traditional beliefs and the gendered division of labor.

Against this historical background, a group appeared whose work and lives were deeply imprinted with gender inequality: family dependents (*jiashu*). In the *danwei*, workers and dependents worked and lived together "to make workers' living more convenient and to benefit production."[8] The *danwei* thus carried out the functions of both production and social reproduction. Over 1.6 million dependents lived in industrial work units in China at the end of 1951.[9] The number increased to over 4.3 million in 1956.[10]

Family dependent was an officially recognized social status in the Mao era.[11] More than eleven thousand dependents' committees were established in the *danwei*.[12] Over 1,300 dependents attended the First National Dependents' Congress in Beijing in June 1957, and so did major party leaders, including Mao Zedong. At the event, Lai Ruoyu, the president of the All-China Federation of Trade Unions, spoke of dependents as "a part of the working class."[13] Three months later, at the Third National Women's Congress, the relations between workers and dependents were defined as "not only family" but "comrades who build a new socialist life together."[14]

Not all dependents were seen positively. In 1956–57, because of problems arising from the expansion of mutual-aid teams in some rural areas, the women affected were eager to leave their villages. Many wives moved to the cities to reunite with husbands working at urban factories. The government criticized these women's individual migrations as "countercurrent" and pushed them to move back to their home villages.[15] But the workers put pressure on their cadres to support their wives' staying in the city. As a compromise, dependents were organized to work in mutual-aid or small production teams: farming and husbandry, laundry and sewing, and supplementary production in their husbands' work units. Whether or not these jobs were paid, they were officially designated as housework, and the logic was that they supported the families and thus advanced industrial production.[16] This definition of housework was quite broad. It included commonly understood domestic work, handicrafts, collective agricultural production, and part-time participation in industrial manufacturing. All of these jobs were acknowledged and seen as valid contributions to the socialist economy. Work inside and outside the home was seen as closely related. It is notable that domestic labor was included, because soon it would not be.

In 1958, the Great Leap Forward recruited some three million women to the urban factories. Most of them were workers' wives from the countryside.[17] The party line changed: women's participation in industrial production mattered more than their housework.[18] One material example of this ideological shift was that some work units started offering overnight childcare, enabling women to work at night.[19]

When the Great Leap Forward collapsed and the economy contracted in 1961, the state laid off millions of laborers. The number of female employees in state factories dropped from ten million in 1960 to six million in 1963.[20] Those laid off were encouraged to return to the countryside to perform farming or domestic work, but many women stayed with their husbands in the cities.[21] Many work units established dependents' production teams: these workers were officially registered as "dependent workers," a status between dependent and worker, but commonly just called "dependents." Their role in the production was considered supplementary, consisting of tasks like raw-material preparation or sideline production. Women's "second shift"—domestic work and childcare—disappeared from the official discourse.

These shifting definitions and valuations of the labor of dependent workers reflected the central government's changing judgments about domestic labor and housewives. Many of these judgments were variations of socialist feminist thought. Informed by a philosophy pioneered by Engels and Lenin that considers public production the only path to women's liberation and views household chores as a significant obstacle, some Chinese socialist feminists deprecated domestic care work.[22] From the First National Women's Congress in 1949 to public statements issued by Song Qingling (the widow of Sun Yat-sen and the vice chair of the Central Government of the

People's Republic of China) and other party leaders in 1950, housewives were described as "parasites" and housework as "trivial things" that "restrained and stifled women, and made women stupid and conservative."[23]

By contrast, a public statement of the All-China Women's Federation (ACWF) in 1952 recommended that "we avoid disparaging domestic labor while encouraging public employment, and clarify the importance of domestic labor to housewives so they can be content with doing housework."[24] Work units were directed by the government "to save enough time for the dependents to do housework." Cai Chang, the ACWF president, delivered a speech at the First National Dependents' Congress in 1957 in which she claimed, "All kinds of labor that contribute to the socialist project are honorable," and "Housework contributes to the socialist project, and it is necessary in order to build socialism." Keeping one foot in each camp, Cai Chang stated that while housework contributed to the socialist society, the ultimate goal of women's emancipation was participation in productive work outside the home.[25] Furthermore, there were two ACWF-led "Diligence and Thrift for Country and Family" campaigns in the 1950s and '60s touting domestic labor.

The voices calling for the valuing of women's domestic labor faded after 1964 as a side effect of a campaign initiated by Mao Zedong against some regional attempts to allow the rural collectives to divide and lease agricultural fields to individual households. Mao claimed that these attempts veered away from socialist collectivization and toward capitalist privatization and called for a stop to all activities that appear to foster private enterprise. Mao's campaign was waged mainly in the domains of economics and production. However, some party members steered it toward the social and political domains. Two official publications of the Central Committee of the Communist Party, *Red Flag* and *People's Daily*, published articles criticizing discussions of domestic labor and other gender-related issues as a way to promote the "private sector" and to separate women's liberation from the proletarian revolution. This official discourse deemed class as the sole reasonable analytic in the public debate over Chinese socialist development.[26]

These central government voices were influential. Thus when the rural Shandongese women reunited with their husbands, or when they married men working in the wood industry in Fujian, domestic labor had already become completely invisible in official discourse, which asserted that urban men and women could create value for the socialist economy only through public production. Therefore, dependents' domestic labor was neither compensated nor acknowledged. Because of their assigned roles within the family, women's labor was ripe for exploitation: their contributions at home and in the factories could be unpaid, underpaid, and exploited in the service of the socialist China's project of capital accumulation.

Rural Women as a Reserve Army of Labor

Xiaomei means little sister. Xiaomei was the youngest of seven children in her rural Shandongese household. When she began working at the Dragon Lake Forest Farm in the early 1960s, at the age of nineteen, she was among the youngest and thus continued to be called Xiaomei. I first met her in 2014, on the third anniversary of her husband's death. Xiaomei talked a lot about him, always in praise. He was a brave, tireless logger and supportive at home. "The one who held the baby while eating meals was always him. I never did it." Xiaomei clearly remembered this detail and was very appreciative of their decades-long marriage.

When the government notified the Shandongese workers in 1960 that their two-year stays in Fujian were to become permanent, married men were allowed to invite their wives and children to reunite with them in Fujian, and single men to seek wives back in their home regions. To encourage the wives to migrate, the government promised them decent living conditions. The government's rationale, in the official phrase recalled by many workers, was to "stabilize the workers' emotion and production." Here *workers* meant male workers only. The government sought to smooth industrial production by separating women from their land and moving them 1,500 kilometers to fulfill male workers' social and sexual needs and to provide them with free domestic labor.

Promising to fulfill men's needs for wives was a Chinese Communist Party (CCP) tradition. In the 1930s and 1940s, China had witnessed a crisis among patriarchal rural families when male peasants could not afford brides, and female peasants who were carrying more economic responsibility than before increasingly resisted and abandoned their husbands.

The CCP took advantage of this family crisis in its mass mobilization of the peasantry to join the Red Army. On the one hand, the CCP attempted to redefine family roles to be less restrictive and more egalitarian so that women could participate in the revolution. On the other hand, it also carefully nurtured patriarchal sentiments and implicitly promised a restoration of the traditional peasant family economy: giving men land and wives. In the early 1950s, the party used the same tactic in the Land Reform Movement. Even though the CCP persuaded women to support land reform, the land was distributed to families, not individuals. As a result, male interests were not threatened.[27]

Following this tradition, the government permitted the Shandongese men to bring their wives to Fujian in the early 1960s. This measure achieved several goals at the same time: maintaining the traditional patriarchal family, satisfying male laborers' sexual and social needs, and enlisting cheaper female laborers. This discourse centered men's needs and concealed the fact that women also provided cheap labor for the enterprises.

Xiaomei's husband, one of the Shandong loggers, returned to his township at age thirty to seek a wife. He was put in touch with Xiaomei's family through acquaintances. For a nineteen-year-old woman from an impoverished family, an "old bachelor" with a stable job was seen as a good match, so she married him and came to Fujian.[28] The second day after she arrived at the Dragon Lake Forest Farm, Xiaomei was assigned to the dependents production team, made up of many newly arrived wives.

Farm tasks were clearly divided between the male state workers and the female dependent workers. Men cut down trees and transported logs. Xiaomei and other women worked alongside the male loggers to cut branches and peel the bark from logs, create fire breaks, and burn the clear-cut areas to prepare the soil for the next round of planting. The women went on to plant trees in spring, following the Lunar New Year: digging holes, tilling the soil, and applying fertilizer. These women still remember the metrics that ruled these tasks: the distance between two pine trees was supposed to be 1 meter, and between fir trees 1.2 meters. A row of broadleaf trees was planted between every three to five rows of conifers, and the distance between two broadleaf trees was supposed to be about one meter more than between conifers. Each female worker could plant fifty to sixty young trees every day, depending on how steep the slope was, and about three thousand trees every spring. Over the next three years, they returned in the spring and summer to clear underbrush and grass to help the young trees grow. When the trees were three years old and their roots were established, they applied fertilizer.

Dependent workers' jobs were time-consuming and detail oriented. Xiaomei commented, "If the [state] workers worked on the mountain for one day, we dependents needed to follow them and work in the same spot for three days." The work changed with the seasons. She continued, "It was so bitter. We went to work before 8 a.m., with a tin box of steamed rice and a bowl of prepared food. We always ate meals in the mountains. We went out in the morning and came back after the day got dark. Sometimes it was too dark to see anything. It was so much work for us dependents. We worked every day regardless of the weather, except for the rainiest days. If the logging camp assigned us to take charge of this mountain, we had to finish it."

Because vehicles were scarce, trucks were used only to transport timber. Workers had to walk from their satellite living quarters to the mountain worksites, which might be three to eight kilometers away—involving two to five hours of rough walking each day. The dependents' jobs involved a lot of manual work—for example, peeling off tree bark and pulling out roots. They used hoes to break up soil and dig holes. They grasped tall grass or small plants with one hand while cutting them with a sickle in the other. They recalled that their work gloves were often worn out and needed to be stitched up or replaced. So did shoes and pants, which became torn and damaged from lots of mountain climbing.

Although laborious, the dependents' tasks were not compensated in the same way as men's logging and transporting work. State workers received stable monthly salaries of about ¥40. Dependent workers were paid based on the number and productivity of their workdays, earning ¥30 to ¥50 per month. Every worker was assigned a quota for the day's task. For example, each might be required to cut off and gather twenty-five kilograms of branches. Meeting the quota would earn a worker the full number of daily work points, which were worth ¥1.5. Consequently their income varied depending on the season and number of workdays in the month. For a couple of months each year, when dependents were assigned to work every day without a break, they very likely earned more than their husbands. But in most months, their salaries were lower than the men's.

Meanwhile, all workers were allocated rations of grains and other material goods, but the state workers were given more than the dependents because it was assumed that men would share food and goods with their wives and children. Here are the monthly rice rations for different groups in Shaowu's state forestry in the mid-1970s:

State worker: 45 *jin* (22.5 kilograms)
Dependent: 23 *jin* (11.5 kilograms), plus 0.2 *jin* (0.1 kilograms) on each working day
Adolescent: 18 *jin* (9 kilograms)
Young child: 7 *jin* (3.5 kilograms)

This materialization of cultural assumptions about gender roles did not match the reality in which men and women alike bore heavy and difficult workloads.

Stories of work hazards, injuries, and deaths abounded in the forest farm community. The workers remembered and often talked about male workers who were killed by fallen trees or truck crashes on winding mountain roads. They also recollected the danger and fear that female workers endured, as their tasks brought them into contact with creatures such as snakes and hornets. When telling me about these experiences, they became animated and emphasized the posttraumatic feelings they still had decades later. Xiaomei told me the following story with her shoulders and chest slightly hunched, her head and face covered with both hands, and her eyes closed.

There was tall grass in the woods, and we had to push it aside by hand in order to move forward. There were a lot of hornets. When we whacked the grass, sometimes we hit hornet nests. We lay down, covered our faces with our bamboo hats, didn't dare to make any sound, and hid until all the hornets left. Once I heard a woman screaming, and after I ran to see her, she had already gotten many dark hornet stings on her body and a swollen, bruised tongue. Several of us slowly carried her back home and called a doctor to treat her. After that, she refused to go back into the mountains. She was too scared. Some people died from the hornet stings too.

Like *xiaomei*, *laoniang* is a familial term in Chinese. It means "maternal grandmother" in some northern regions, including Shandong. My reason for calling the woman in the next story Laoniang is more personal: my mother asked me to. Before I met Laoniang to hear her story, my mother explained that when she was growing up and working at the Shaowu Sawmill, Laoniang treated her like a daughter. Laoniang often made delicious Shandong-style steamed buns and fried flatbread. If my mother dropped by her apartment on the way to school or work, Laoniang always gave her a snack.

When I first moved back to the Shaowu Sawmill living quarters in 2013, Laoniang heard me introduce myself as Baozhu's daughter. She commented that I had changed a lot and warmly invited me to have a meal at her place. She made flatbread and told me about her favorite grandson, who was attending college. Laoniang ended up being the first dependent worker with whom I did a life history interview. When I began requesting formal videotaped interviews with the dependent workers, after I had spent three months among them, all of them gave negative responses like "Don't interview me. I'm illiterate. I don't know how to tell a story, and my story is not worth listening to." They redirected me to interview the cadres or state workers. Laoniang alone agreed to an interview, mostly because she wanted to help me complete my book. After she described the interview to other dependents, some of them followed her lead.

During our interview, Laoniang talked about her chronic body aches and attributed them to the physical hardship she had endured during her work at the sawmill. Two years after our interview, Laoniang passed away. I mailed a video copy of our three-hour interview to her family, hoping that the people she loved, including her favorite grandson, would watch and remember the stories that mattered to her.

When the Japanese army invaded Shandong in 1937 and 1938, Laoniang was about eight. Poverty and hunger struck her family. She picked up vegetable waste at the markets and boiled it to eat with salt. Occasionally some kind-hearted person gave her a flatbread, and she brought it to her grandmother, who had bound feet and could not walk far.[29] Even so, Laoniang envied the girls from wealthy families who could bind their feet. Her family was too poor to have cloth for shoes and clothes, much less for foot binding. Laoniang walked a long way barefoot, and in winter, she made herself shoes from straw. Her feet were still cold. "My childhood was very bitter," she commented. "It was in the old society" (meaning the time before the Communist revolution). She showed me a deep, two-inch-long scar on her belly: "Once the Japanese came, and we all hid in a mine. I'm not sure if it was from the dust or poison, but my belly was very swollen." The skin broke open later. She continued: "I was short of breath and almost died. My grandma cried so hard. I survived in the end, but my right shoulder, arm, and hand all went bad." She showed me her right hand and its crooked index finger.

> My old man and I married [in an arranged marriage] when I was nine-
> teen. I delivered three kids in 1952, 1954, and 1957. My old man came
> to Fujian in 1958. At that time, people were afraid of snakes in Fujian,
> so I did not want to go. He served in the militia and Communist Youth
> League, so he went to take the lead [to encourage others to go]. After he
> left, I had to take care of three kids on my own, while still going to work
> in the fields. They [the people's commune] did not give food to people
> who did no work. That winter was so cold. I locked the kids at home
> and brought a pot to pick up food [from the communal canteen]. My
> feet were wet, and I almost could not continue working. Ah, but I lived
> through all this bitterness.

Rural Chinese women were exhausted by their double burden of participating in the collective work of people's communes and continuing their domestic work. And because infant mortality rates substantially decreased in the 1950s, due to government-directed training for midwives and improved hygiene conditions, women had more children to care for.[30]

Laoniang finally joined her husband at the Shaowu Sawmill in 1960 and was registered as a dependent worker. Like many industries after the Great Leap Forward, the sawmill laid off most women in 1962 and directed them to return home. Laoniang dreaded a return to village life as a single mother. Her neighbor Rong, a state worker, was also laid off and voiced her anger. But soon news came that Chiang Kai-shek's Nationalist Army would attack the mainland with Fujian as the first target. Frightened, Laoniang and Rong took their children back to Shandong, leaving their husbands in Fujian. When three years had passed and the Nationalist attack did not materialize, Fujian was believed to be safe again. In 1966, many women workers returned to Shaowu, and this time all the women were recruited into the dependents production team, regardless of their former status as state workers or dependents.

A popular narrative described workers in socialist China as having "iron rice bowls," meaning permanent employment. This narrative was partial and masculinized. Paid labor for women was unstable and periodic, although many women, especially male workers' wives, performed small tasks for the work units even when they were not officially hired and paid. During industrialization and economic development projects such as the Great Leap Forward, women were hired and paid. But when the projects ended and the broader economy contracted, women were laid off at a disproportionately higher rate than men.[31]

Rural women in particular were the reserve army of labor for the urban industries.[32] Their poor living conditions, caused by disadvantageous grain rationing and household registration systems, compelled rural women to leave their native land and take urban jobs. Even though their work in the cities (including the "urbanized" forest farms) was backbreaking, as Laoniang, Xiaomei, and Zhuang Jinxian all tried to convey, the general living and working conditions were still better than in the countryside. Thus, despite offering women lower pay and status as well as poorer job security than men received, the state could quickly recruit these laid-off workers again.

Underpaid Women's Work

Women's status as the reserve army of labor also manifested in their deployment in seasonal and on-demand labor and frequent transfers between positions, even when they were hired to work in the same units as men. A state worker of either gender had a fixed position in the workshop. For instance, a state worker who removed knots from boards very likely kept doing that same job until retirement. However, women dependent workers were treated very differently. They worked indoors and out, frequently being reassigned to different tasks. Laoniang, for example, would be called to fill temporary openings in the workshop. She stacked thin layers of wood to be glued together for plywood, repaired the filter for the wood waste used in making particleboard, did quality control at the end of the assembly line, and also climbed up the side of a three-story-high tank to throw in raw materials at the beginning of the assembly line. One might argue that Laoniang deserved higher pay than her state-worker counterparts, since she did so many jobs on the assembly line and knew the whole process. However, that was not how jobs and skills were valued. State workers who held one position for a long time were believed to possess a special skill at that task. Dependents doing all the "random" tasks were considered versatile, but not skilled. In other words, their versatility was not valued.

The low value placed on dependents' work was reflected in pay inequities. The state sawmill workers, like those on the forest farm, had fixed monthly salaries, which were scaled primarily according to seniority and ranged from ¥30 to ¥50 in the 1960s and 1970s. Laoniang and other dependents received a monthly paycheck based on the number of days worked. The sawmill paid Laoniang ¥1 per working day. The dependents production team took 10 percent as a "management fee," which paid for a dependent worker's straw hat and rain cape, oversleeves, and towels. The state workers got these work clothes for free. Dependents also received fewer rationed goods than state workers.

Once a temporary opening that Laoniang was filling in the workshop was given to a state worker, she was reassigned, typically returning to where she was "supposed" to be: outdoors. Most of Laoniang's work involved delivering materials to the various workshops and yards. She moved railway ties, sawdust, and coal in a two-wheeled cart that she moved with her left shoulder—the one that had survived her childhood illness undamaged.

When asked about the gendered nature of tasks at the sawmill, workers of both genders told me that men were stronger and thus could do "heavy" jobs, while women could only do "light" work. But once you know the details of the jobs, this explanation falls apart. In the manufacture of railroad ties, male state workers transported the logs from trucks to the workshop by hand and using cranes, and then male and female state workers processed them into scaled railway ties. Women dependents hand-carried the finished ties to load them into train cars. As Laoniang's description shows, this "light" job" was arguably among the most physically demanding jobs in the sawmill.

> We dependents worked, while the workers were working; when they
> left work, we still kept working, moving products to trains. Trains often
> came at night, so we worked at night, carrying the railroad ties and put-
> ting them into the train cars. . . . We carried the railroad ties up to the
> train by walking up a wooden plank leading up to the top of the train.
> The top of the train was so tall! As tall as a one-story building. We two
> women carried a railway tie weighing more than one hundred *jin*. The
> plank was not wide, either. Poor us, working in that kind of dangerous
> situation! Sometimes, the ties got wet with rain, and they got stuck on
> our shoulders and thus were really hard to throw into the train. If you
> didn't work, you didn't have money; but if you worked, you felt scared.
> If the ties fell on your head, you would lose your life. Have you ever seen
> the ties? Two and a half meters long and 240 [millimeters] wide. When
> two of us carried a tie, we could not even see each other.

Why were the supposedly weaker women assigned to carry out these physically demanding tasks? Despite the official distinction between "heavy" and "light" jobs, I found that the division depended much more on whether tasks involved the use of machinery. The more machinery was involved, the more difficult and skilled a task was considered to be, and the more likely that it would assigned to a male worker. If a task was accomplished by hand, it was assumed that no intellectual work was needed, and therefore a woman could "simply" finish it. For example, the plywood workshop, which required more manual labor, employed more women workers than the particleboard workshop, which relied more on machinery. All the electricians and repair workers were male.

The perception that women are "only" good at working with materials, and not with machines, exists across a variety of cultural and geographical contexts. The idea is that men possess higher technological aptitude, while women are assumed to be more patient and careful and to have "nimble fingers."[33] In industrialization worldwide, the increasing use of machines, mainly by men, has been considered a sign of progress. The term *technology* has become largely interchangeable with *machinery*. This monolithic understanding of skills, technology, and modernization has enabled discrimination against women and exploitation of their labor.

The division of labor in the state wood industry in the Mao era can be represented as a set of concentric circles. Work that used machinery and yielded immediate products occupied center, signifying the most advanced form of socialist industrialization. This included logging and assembly-line work done by the mostly male state workers, who accordingly received stable employment and fixed benefits. (Women, in fact, also did this kind of work, either as unusual examples of state workers, like Zhuang Jinxian, or as temporary workers, like Laoniang, but their work was not acknowledged.)

In the next circle was the underpaid productive work done by female manual laborers, which might not result in immediate products and profits. These jobs included cleaning up after logging, planting new crops, and moving raw materials and products. Seen as secondary to socialist development, these jobs could be swiftly abolished if the project ran into difficulties.

The outermost circle, consisting of unpaid domestic and care work, was also occupied by women. Domestic labor was not considered valuable for the socialist economy during most of the Maoist era; in fact, after the mid-1960s, the topic disappeared from the party narrative.

Women's labor was essential to sustaining the state wood industry but did not produce short-term yields. It takes decades to grow a baby into human power for the labor market, and decades for a tree to mature into harvestable timber. Domestic work and planting were both essential for sustaining the state wood industry. The unseen, unrecognized products of women's exhausting and unceasing labor were thus expropriated by the state and accumulated as capital.

Unpaid Women's Work

Xiaomei had four children. The village midwives assisted in her four home births, after each of which she required hospitalization in urban Shaowu. Therefore, she was always scared during pregnancy. The birth was not only a physical and emotional burden but also a financial one. Because dependents were paid by the day, the leave that Xiaomei took before and after childbirth reduced her income and her ration of goods and food, a loss that was particularly devastating during pregnancy. Her postpartum illnesses resulted in chronic health problems. But the health risks and physical harms of pregnancy and labor were not considered workplace hazards, so they were not compensated by her work unit. Having borne four daughters, Xiaomei was worried and almost put one up for adoption, a common practice for girls-only families at that time. Working in an unfamiliar environment as a recent migrant, going through pregnancy and labor, and raising four daughters in a society with marked gender inequalities—all were daunting jobs for this working mother, and all were invisible and unpaid. "We [the logging camp workers] were not very careful in child rearing in general," she said. "We usually brought lunch to the mountains, because many hills were steep and the work areas were far away. We did not return until the evenings. There was leftover flatbread or rice porridge at home for the kids. Older ones helped take care of the younger ones. The workers who didn't go into the mountains that day would keep an eye on the kids as well. If the working area that day was nearby, we would come home, washing clothes or doing other chores."

Women's inclusion in the paid labor force did not necessarily liberate them or remove domestic and professional gender inequalities. Paid work outside the home was simply added to women's disproportionately high load of unpaid domestic work.[34] Women like Xiaomei carried heavy duties inside and outside the home, and their assignment to the dependents production team sapped time and energy from their domestic care work. In the late 1960s, ten years after the Dragon Lake Forest Farm had been established, it finally built canteens, nurseries, and schools, which reduced the child-rearing stress on mothers and older children.

"We worked day and night. We did all kinds of work," Laoniang told me, and the jobs she did on the shop floor weren't all. The Shaowu Sawmill rented a farm in a nearby village to supply rice and vegetables for the mill canteen.[35] Workers and dependents worked six days a week at the mill, but dependents also worked on the farm on Sundays. Working in the rice paddies, they often encountered leeches on their legs. In addition, Laoniang grew vegetables for her own family — the food ration for a household with only one state worker could not support multiple adolescent children — so she often needed to water and fertilize the vegetable field after work. Fortunately, the children helped.

Furthermore, because the rationed goods provided by the sawmill were minimal, almost all households needed to produce clothing and other items for themselves. In Laoniang's household, with two adults doing heavy work and three growing children, everyone needed new shoes frequently. She often brought materials to her daytime job to stitch into multilayered shoe soles during breaks. Making shoes took a lot of skill, and Laoniang had been doing it all her life. She shared her tips: She always spun hemp fiber into thread at home, to avoid the hot sun outside that would make the fiber brittle. She also licked the thread before stitching to increase its resilience.

Laoniang and other rural girls learned and sharpened these skills as they grew up, watching and imitating their mothers and grandmothers. However, these skills were often regarded as "natural" rather than learned, so they were taken for granted, devalued, and unpaid, and women were punished if they had not "naturally" mastered them. Laoniang remembered that a woman newly married into her village had been beaten for not knowing how to make shoes. Laoniang commented: "It was ridiculous. What was that beating going to do? Make her able to make shoes? The beating wouldn't teach her to make shoes. So why did they beat her?"

As these women married into other households and even moved to other provinces to perform industrial labor, they were still required to carry out skilled but unpaid tasks like these for their families.

Working around the clock and being constantly busy was the collective experience of Chinese women during early socialist industrialization. Cold War propaganda in the United States touted capitalism as providing more mechanical aid for American housewives, and the Soviet Union and East Germany highlighted the ability of Communism to supply women with equal access to home appliances.[36] In these countries, economic development and better living standards meant that women, as citizen consumers, could acquire better tools for domestic work. In China, however, Mao declared: "To liberate women is not to manufacture washing machines."[37]

Instead, Chinese state rhetoric promised material abundance in the public realm, to be achieved via collective labor rather than consumerism. The base of China's industrial development was so weak that pursuing rapid industrialization and mass production meant putting all its resources into heavy industry and limiting investments elsewhere. Individuals and households were compelled to "temporarily" cut their living costs and reduce consumption so that the whole country could pool resources to "quickly" achieve modernization and industrialization. The timeline was left vague, and the level of underconsumption varied between rural and urban, male and female.

Oral histories of rural women reveal extreme austerity and overwork as the norm during the collective period (from 1954 until about 1980).[38] For instance, rural citizens' rations for cotton clothes and other goods were half those of urban dwellers; they had barely enough everyday clothing to wash and change regularly. Rationed goods still had to be paid for, and many people could not afford to claim even their basic allocation. To meet the high and deeply politicized cotton cultivation quotas of village collectives, women had to work sixteen hours or more—and then spin and weave at home to provide clothing and linens.[39] Given the grueling nature of village life, it is perhaps not surprising that rural women were willing to be moved into urban industrialization as an on-demand and cheaper labor force.[40]

Considering domestic and care labor as natural to women was not unique to socialist China.[41] The socialist economy merely continued a patriarchal family tradition that had taken advantage of women's labor by calling it "help."[42] The incentive of high productivity motivated the state economy to preserve old patriarchal gender divisions.[43]

In the context of socialist China's aim to rapidly industrialize and boost production, domestic and care labor was always secondary to productive work. A strong state discourse connected women's liberation with industrial and agricultural production. What women themselves believed would lead to "liberation" is a far more complicated question. When resources for elder- and childcare facilities were channeled into industrial production, women were directed to support production by taking on more work in the home. When more and cheaper labor was needed, women were directed to support production by shouldering more work outside the home. In both cases, women remained responsible for their "natural" role of performing domestic labor.

The integration of industrial (or public) and domestic (or private) spaces in work units in urban China rendered domestic labor contributions mostly invisible. For the most part, work units offered domestic care support only when the lack of it would disrupt production—and the bar was very high, particularly in the early years of socialist development, when underconsumption was a crucial strategy for accumulating capital. As long as women could absorb the demands of care work, even if it meant exhausting themselves, the work units would not step in to provide assistance.

THREE

ALIENATION

I was afraid it would be awkward when Huang Zheng-e volunteered to take me to the Dragon Lake State Forest Farm in 2014. Huang was still an authoritative figure in Dragon Lake Village eight years after her six-year tenure as village head had ended. I had been hearing about conflicts between the farm and the village resulting from the state-enforced lease of the village forests to the farm beginning in the late 1950s. I worried that Huang's presence could put my fieldwork at the farm at risk, but I couldn't bring myself to refuse her kind offer.

The farm director, Zhang, brewed locally grown Lapsang Souchong tea to welcome us and readily agreed to host me after Huang's brief introduction: "This is my cousin's kid." (I am not.) At the meeting, they discussed problems common to the farm and the village, mostly related to the fact that their forests had been categorized as "ecological public benefits forests" in the early 2000s, thereby triggering logging bans. Zhang and Huang then strategized on how to work together to request the county and prefecture to raise the amount of "ecological compensation" to which both the farm and the village were entitled. I was surprised at how friendly the representatives of the forest farm and village were toward each other and how they collaborated to maximize the quantifiable value of the forests.

Most of the peasant families had lived in the Fujian mountains and relied on the forest's resources for generations when the newly established Communist regime indefinitely transferred management and control of a large portion of the forests to state forest farms in 1958. Apparently the hostility of those years had abated by the time I began my fieldwork in the area in 2013. The explanation might be that the peasants had gained rights to manage and commercialize timber around the year 2000, placing them on a par with the forest farms. More important, however, was the increasing alienation of the peasants from the forests as a result of forest reforms from the 1950s onward. Forests went from being a crucial part of the peasants' natural and cultural environment, as well as a source of survival, to being economic assets defined by how much revenue they could bring in. When I conducted fieldwork in Fujian between 2013 and 2018, the conversations I heard between the representatives of the state wood industry and the villages were mostly about how to cash in on these assets.

The oral history of Huang Zheng-e, who lived the roles of ordinary peasant, wood business owner, and village leader between the 1960s and 2010s, represents the perspective of the peasants, whose livelihoods and culture were bound up with the forests. Her shifting views and lived experiences demonstrate how the peasants changed their ways of using, valuing, and relating to the forests. These changes were so profound that most peasants moved out of their villages and away from the forests in the first decade of the twenty-first century. Huang's life story as a peasant turned timber-business owner, who now often needs to negotiate with the state and who hires southwestern rural migrants as her employees, exemplifies the shifting relationship between the peasants and the forests and the process of capital accumulation in the post-Mao forestry industry in Fujian.[1]

Forests as Integral to Culture

In the Qing dynasty (1644–1911), forestland in Fujian was managed according to agreements between tenants and landlords. Because many landlords lived far away in the coastal cities, the peasant tenants had a high degree of freedom over the management of the land and forests. It was implicitly understood that the land was not mere property but also a source of local people's livelihoods, so the peasants hunted, gathered, grew crops, and grazed animals.[2] Attempts by the Republican Chinese government (1911–1948) to control tree cultivation and trade through government-led afforestation and regulation programs had only a short and limited impact.[3]

So the peasants' use of forest resources with limited government regulation persisted until the Communist regime.

After the Communists collectivized the forestland in the 1950s and in some places (including Shaowu) put large portions of it under the management of the state logging camps, peasants still depended on the forest for subsistence. They collected firewood, used timber for home construction, planted vegetables, grazed animals in open areas, and gathered fungi, medicinal plants, and wild fruits and vegetables. In short, the everyday interactions between the peasants and the forests stayed almost unchanged. State policy did affect the peasants' activities to some extent. For example, intentional burning had been banned in Fujian in the 1950s. However, to meet their families' needs, peasants continued the practice in some areas in order to kill weeds, clear land for taro cultivation, and promote the growth of bracken ferns, the rhizomes of which were an even more important source of dietary starch than rice in the northern Fujianese mountains.[4]

The villagers' dependence on the forest to supply daily needs occasionally had tragic consequences. Born in a Fujianese village called Headwater in 1962, Huang Zheng-e had a childhood marked by scarcity. Her family and fellow villagers relied on dispersed, small-scale agriculture and foraging in the forests. One day the nine-year-old Huang, together with two other girls, went to collect tree bark in the forest near her village for fuel. They saw some bright red fruit on plants growing along the ground. The girls thought this fruit looked like the wild berries they always gathered from the forest, so they ate some. The berries were poisonous, and one girl died. Huang survived but missed three years of school because of temporary learning disabilities resulting from the poisoning. Though this instance was tragic, intimate connections with flora and fauna were part of daily life for these children and their families. The close relationship between villagers and forests was sustained through the early 1980s.

In 1979, when Huang was seventeen, her family arranged for her to marry into a Dragon Lake Village household. In 1981, the village gave her household a small plot of private household forestland (*ziliu shan*) under a provincial program that gave residents permanent ownership of parcels of some scattered forestland and barren land around houses.[5] Few village households cultivated these plots. Huang's family planted new tree crops on theirs but did not tend them at all. Huang remembered only one elder committed to tree cultivation. The peasants were reluctant to invest effort in these plots because, given the recent sudden changes in land ownership policies, they worried that the government might reclaim the land. In addition, regardless of ownership, the villagers had always used the land and trees around their homes to meet their basic needs. The indifference of the peasants toward the plots they were allocated provides a good illustration of their relationship to the forests: they saw them as a source of subsistence, not income.[6]

It was because the peasants understood the forests as an integral part of their living environment and culture that they vigorously resisted the state wood industry's logging and processing operations in the 1970s and 1980s. Huang elaborated on a tactic called capping (*dai mao*) that the villagers used to disrupt the state forest farm's logging. They stopped the forest farm from logging the trees on the top third of the mountains, leaving a "cap" for each mountain. In her 2014 interview with me, Huang used ecology-oriented scientific language to explain why a cap was important: the trees at the top of the mountains absorbed water and preserved the mountain springs that provided the village's water. But in the 1970s, when the villagers requested that the state forest farms incorporate capping when setting logging boundaries, they were mostly motivated by a local feng shui belief that every mountain needed a cap of trees.

This was not an isolated case. Chinese villages often invoked traditional ecological or cultural knowledge to resist logging, preserving feng shui forests even during the peak of logging activities in socialist China.[7] Feng shui forests are believed to be beneficial because of their particular location in relation to villages and to natural features such as rivers, mountains, and hills. It is remarkable that using feng shui as a tactic to resist indiscriminate state logging succeeded at a time when feng shui was stigmatized as a product of feudalism and superstition and was suppressed and marginalized by the Communist Party.

The tactics to stop the logging, though, went beyond cultural beliefs. To explain how Huang's village stopped the state from logging the mountain caps, Huang educated me about the local topography and divisions of the forests. In northern Fujian, administrative village headquarters were mostly located at the base of mountains. Paved public roads usually went through the administrative villages. "First-layer" mountains (*yi chong shan*) were the mountains closest to the administrative villages, near the roads. Second-layer mountains (*er chong shan*) lay farther away. In the 1970s and 1980s, the state logging camps managed the forests of the second- and third-layer mountains, while the villages controlled the first layer. This division became the basis of Dragon Lake Village's leverage in their negotiations with the logging camp.

"If they didn't agree to our proposal of capping, we would completely stop them from logging," Huang explained. "We would block the roads in the first-layer mountains, which were owned by us villagers. Then their trucks would not be able to get into their mountains. If they had no transportation, their production work would be stopped." It was of course illegal for the villagers to block public roads. However, the forest farms, the government, and the police would have no immediate practical recourse against such action. Many corners of rural China are beyond the reach of law enforcement. Certainly the higher-level authorities could put pressure on village leaders. However, the village leaders might invoke the cultural belief of feng shui to justify the action and explain the difficulty of preventing it. Such tactics compelled the forest farm to take into account the values of local communities.

Trees as a Commodity

In the mid-1980s, local values began to change. The state monopoly on timber was abolished, and the market opened up.[8] The Fujian provincial government allowed village collectives to log trees and sell timber and small pieces of lumber. But the villages were permitted to sell the wood only to the Shaowu State Sawmill, just as the forest farms did. The sawmill then coordinated wood sales to the regional and national markets. The idea, informed by the new capitalist market economy, was to stabilize prices and preserve the forests while also motivating villagers to participate in the trade. This policy changed the peasants' relationship to the forests. Instead of seeing trees as part of the fabric of their living environment, they began to assess their exchange value.

Under the new policy, individuals could grow tree crops on their own small plots and sell standing trees around their houses for profit. In 1986, Huang, along with her husband and brother-in-law, began planting crops of China fir and Chinese red pine and selling the seedlings for replanting in other provinces. They used the money for their children's education (or, in Huang's words, for "cultivating the children"). Huang paid extra to send her children to a middle school in urban Shaowu with better resources and teachers. In 1998, when her daughter had gone to college, Huang and her husband started a wood product business in Shanghai and left their son at school in urban Shaowu. After twelve years in the wood business, she had earned enough to improve her family's living conditions, which involved leaving the village. Commodifying the trees went hand in hand with physically removing peasants from the forests.

A mainstream narrative about the condition of Chinese forests could be summarized as follows. The forests were devastated during the 1950s and 1970s because of massive deforestation and resource exploitation by the Communist regime. Most parts of Maoist China characterized the forests as "free goods," like coal deposits. Under the planned economy, procurement prices between different units of the state-operated wood industry were set at a very low, fixed rate. Labor costs were low because workers were underpaid. The consequences were overcutting and waste along all the links of the industrial chain. The capitalist reform saved the forests by implementing reforestation and forest-conservation policies and programs. Since then, China has achieved globally recognized success in increasing its forested area.[9]

This narrative, however, omits many complications. First, deforestation had been taking place for centuries, particularly during the Qing and Republican eras. The CCP's approach to forestry was a continuation of this earlier history.[10] Second, although China's forest volume increased greatly after the 1970s, species diversity declined, because biologically diverse old-growth forests had been harvested, and new plantings consisted of just one or a few species.[11] Third, forest-conservation policies changed significantly after the 1998 floods on the Yangtze River and three other major Chinese rivers. The Chinese central government had implemented many reforestation and forest-conservation projects in the 1980s and 1990s. After the 1985 Forest Law stipulated that forest logging must not outpace natural growth, the National Forestry Administration established logging quotas for each province.[12] After the floods, the government extended these efforts, which had centered on afforestation and logging regulations, to include the downsizing of state forest farms and the privatization of collectively owned forests.

The floods in the summer of 1998 killed several thousand people and adversely affected over two hundred million. Both the international environmentalist community and Chinese official discourse blamed deforestation for the floods.[13] But the concerns of the Chinese government went beyond the environmental harms. The Yangtze Basin produced 39.3 percent of China's GDP in 1995, as well as a huge amount of the nation's food. Nearly five million houses were destroyed, and the direct economic loss was about ¥166 billion.[14] It would be cheaper to prevent flooding by subsidizing forest protection and expansion than to rebuild all the infrastructure and houses that could be damaged by future floods and mudslides.

The measures to prevent deforestation and maximize afforestation included not only changes to forest ownership but also a turn to imports.[15] Deforestation was blamed on the state forest farms and their "inefficient" use of timber, and the farm workforce was downsized. The Dragon Lake Forest Farm, which had had one thousand employees in its heyday, employed only one hundred by the year 2000. Between 2003 and 2004, Fujian province transferred the ownership of the trees in collective-owned forests to households. (The land still belongs to the collectives.)[16] Households are now entitled to sell and lease their land-use rights, sell standing trees, and harvest other forest resources.

These policy changes were informed by the neoliberal economic discourse of efficiency: the defunding of state enterprises and deregulation of industry would allow private business to flourish, and the free market would bring about the most efficient use of the raw materials. In consequence, the forestry industry would need less timber and log fewer trees. The privatization of the wood industry aimed to minimize timber waste and keep deforestation in check.

In 2000, as these changes were taking hold, Huang left her husband and business in Shanghai and came back to Shaowu to take care of her mother-in-law, who had fallen ill. There, she was elected head of Dragon Lake Village, which had become a state-certified "village in poverty." The villagers believed her business experience and ambitious personality could help with development. Although female village heads were not unknown in China, she was the first female leader in Dragon Lake.

One of Huang's main responsibilities was to assist the villagers in increasing their income and improving living conditions. The village's main assets were forest resources. In 2003, Huang applied to the city and prefecture People's Congresses and received a special grant to build a 9.3-kilometer concrete road between her village and the local township's administrative and business center. This enabled the villagers to find more business opportunities and jobs away from the village.[17] An improved transportation route also meant more opportunities to lease the now-privatized forestland and sell timber. The construction of the road thus increased the peasants' participation in the wood trade, which was a major rationale in Huang's grant application.

Huang also took advantage of other natural resources to increase the village's revenue. Dragon Lake Village, along with two other villages, had rented its river to a privately owned hydroelectric station for ¥10,000 per village per year. Huang reached out to the other two villages and negotiated with the power station manager to raise the rent to ¥100,000 per year, split among the three villages. When the manager refused, Huang initiated a withdrawal from the contract. The villages issued a tender for a new renter and were able to name their price: ¥100,000.

Huang did not forget the Dragon Lake State Forest Farm, whose lands had been leased from the villagers when it was established in 1958. If not for those leases, the peasants could have obtained revenue from selling the timber themselves. As matters stood, the farm's rent for some four hundred square kilometers of forestland was one of the village's big revenue sources. From the 1950s until the 1980s, the farm paid a fixed annual rent. In the 1990s, the village pressured the government to switch to a monthly payment that gave the village 20 percent of the net profit from the farm's sales of timber and tree branches. In 2000, Huang managed to increase the village's share of the profit to 30 percent.

In 2001, during the time of forestry privatization and rising environmentalism, Fujian and seven other provinces began officially dividing the forests into "commercial forests" and "ecological public benefit forests."[18] Based on the trees' species, age, volume, girth, and other indicators, as well as their proximity to transportation, this system separates the forests into two categories: those with high ecological value and those whose economic value could be higher than their ecological value. Owners of the ecological public benefit forests are compensated at a fixed amount per *mu* (667 square meters) through a "payment for ecosystem services" (PES) set by the province and prefecture, but these forests are under a full-scale logging ban.[19] Owners of the commercial forests may manage and commodify the trees according to national and provincial logging quotas related to species, girth, and age. In 2018, 70 percent of Fujian's forests were still categorized as commercial.

These metrics and the pricing system shaped how the peasants viewed the forests. In order to negotiate with the state over categorization and compensation, they had to learn the language of tree measurement. As a result, they internalized the understanding of trees as commodities: some create more exchange value than others. Exchange value doesn't always come from putting commodities into a market; compensation may instead result from the opportunity cost of not doing so.

Almost all of the state forest farm's lands and 20 percent of village household-owned forests were categorized as ecological public benefit forests. Depending on the proximity of the forests to transportation routes, most peasants preferred that their forests be defined as commercial forests. In the first decade of the 2000s, the price of timber in the market was much higher than the ecological compensation. But if the forests were in remote locations and transporting the timber would cost too much, or if the forests included too many trees classified as rare species (which peasants were not allowed to log regardless), then the preference shifted toward categorization as ecological public benefit forests. Every time I visited the villages and forest farms between 2013 and 2018, conversation centered on the level of ecological compensation, logging regulations in the commercial forests, and the price of timber for different species and tree sizes. For the peasants whose families had lived with the forests for generations, trees had become commodities.

It was not only the peasants' perspectives on the trees that changed, but their physical relation to them as well. Villagers around Huang's age often recalled their childhood in the 1960s and 1970s with the forests as the backdrop. They gathered vegetables, fruits, and fungi in the forests and brought them home to eat. They collected firewood for home use and caught frogs, fish, and snails in the mountain streams. However, when I visited the villages between 2013 and 2018, most of the peasants had already moved into urban Shaowu. Their homes back in the villages were newly constructed concrete houses with decent interior decoration, but aside from the occasional visit, people didn't spend time there.

Between 1990 and 2000, some peasants began migrating to the big coastal cities seeking employment. They went back and forth between their workplaces in the cities and the villages, leaving their children with grandparents in the villages. By 2010, almost all villages had paved roads leading to the cities. More convenient transportation resulted in an increase in young people from the villages seeking employment in the big cities and in urban Shaowu. With the privatization of forest tenure and increasing wood prices between 2003 and 2008, most villagers "sold" their forests: that is, they rented them out on seventy-year leases. The high price of wood led to lucrative lease terms for the villagers. With the lump-sum leasing fees, many villagers purchased apartments in urban Shaowu, and three generations left the village all together. Some families left the old men in the village, either because these men were not used to living in apartments in the cities or because they were not helpful to the younger family members, whereas the female elders could take care of the grandchildren and assist with chores. When I visited Dragon Lake Village in 2014, only about ten old men were still living there.

Why would the peasants choose to rent out the forestland and move to the city instead of staying and managing the forests for long-term revenue? In addition to the elevated wood prices, there were some historical reasons. Rural China had suffered from extreme underconsumption in the Mao era. Cities provided much better goods and services. During the reforms of the 1970s, official discourse portrayed rural areas as a "cultural desert." Many working-age men and women of rural Shaowu had migrated to the cities in the 1990s. By the time forestry property rights were distributed in the following decade, this generation was not familiar with forest management. On top of that, caring for and logging trees was considered more arduous than a city job. Leasing the forests to others to manage and harvest for a fixed long-term rent looked like a much better idea.

Three groups typically leased forestland from the villagers. The least common were businesspeople from outside the village. Some leases were purchased by villagers who were particularly skilled at farming and tree cultivation and who stayed in the village, renting and managing others' fields and forests. The most common renters, however, were villagers (who might or might not still live in the village) who had trust and influence within the village as well as government connections, and who hired others to do the actual forest work. All three groups of renters leased plots from multiple households so that they could manage large areas of forests as a unit to increase efficiency and revenue. For these renters, control of the forest plots is equivalent to ownership of means of production. Their main concerns are how to increase the timber's exchange value, decrease the cost of production, and maximize capital accumulation.

Huang herself rented and managed plots owned by other village families. Years of experience working for the government as village head had given her connections in the forestry administration, so she heard of policy changes very early and responded to them quickly. She also knew the bureaucratic procedures for submitting logging-permit applications and other aspects of forest management. Huang and her brother-in-law rented forests from twenty households. Like other peasants, Huang had moved to urban Shaowu in 2006 and lived in the city most of the time. Only when she had to monitor tree planting, logging operations, or other projects did she come to her house in the village for a short stay. Although the logging quota was very low and decreasing every year, there was still much work to do in the forests. Huang hired seasonal labor for tree planting and logging.

New Rural Migrants

Logging, planting, and caring for trees are seasonal jobs, so workers need to move every few months. Huang and other forest owners hired rural migrant workers from the southwestern Chinese provinces of Guizhou and Yunnan. These groups first came to Fujian to work in forestry in the 1990s. When the state forest farms laid off the majority of their employees in 2000, they began using these southwestern migrants as on-demand laborers. Later, private forest managers like Huang followed suit. The southwestern workers were thought of as "cheaper" (commanding a lower salary and no benefits), "more productive," and "docile."

The living and working conditions of these migrants were very different from the conditions experienced by those who had worked for the state forest farms before. Their job and housing insecurities were striking. I interviewed eight new migrant workers between 2014 and 2018, two of whom were female. When they first came in the 1990s, they usually built simple sheds to live in, or if they were lucky, they found abandoned village homes to use. By around 2005, almost all the residents of the state forest farm satellite sites had been laid off and had moved to urban areas in search of employment. The new migrant workers or their employers coordinated with the forest farms and got their permission to rent the now-empty camp apartments. These apartments usually had some working electrical outlets, plumbing and water, and sometimes even some worn but usable furniture.

When new migrants showed me their bedrooms and told me that "putting two boards together on top of benches is a bed or a desk for us," I thought of the first-generation state loggers' similar experiences in the late 1950s and early 1960s. But the new migrant workers did not have employee housing and benefits as those state workers did. Nor had the state workers needed to purchase their own tools, clothing, replacement saw blades, gasoline, and so on, as the new migrants did. (Because of the expense of purchasing and maintaining specific equipment, loggers and planters are usually two separate groups.) The new migrants made between ¥30,000 and ¥40,000 a year in the mid- and late 2010s, and the necessary equipment and working clothes could cost over a third of their pay—on top of paying rent.

The eight migrant workers I interviewed included two single and two married men, and two married couples working together. The married men's wives and children stayed in urban Shaowu so the children could attend school. The married couples either left their young children in their home villages with the grandparents or had children old enough to attend

Modifications of state forest farm apartments by southwestern migrant workers, 2018. One converted an old living room into a kitchen by installing an induction cooker, and another created a kitchen area by building two mud stoves outside the apartment and piping water from the apartment through a long hose.

college or work. The interviewees were mostly forty to fifty years old. The sex ratio of my interviewees reflects the ratio between men and women workers in this industry in the late 2010s.

Both of the couples had worked in the export-oriented electronic and shoe factories in big cities until they were "too old to stand up and work thirteen hours every day with almost no break." Because forestry work involves hard and dangerous manual tasks, young people were no longer attracted to the industry. These older workers appreciated what they saw as the freedom of these jobs: because there was no constant supervision and monitoring, the small group of three to eight workers could control their own rhythm of work and breaks, provided they finished the assigned tasks within the two or three months allotted. Men and women working on a team in the 2010s usually divided the compensation equally. In the 1990s and early 2000s, women had earned less, as they had only been doing "cleanup" tasks.

When I interviewed them, these workers had developed trusting relationships with the locals, including state and private forest business owners and managers, after working for them for a decade or more. Yet they remembered the many times they had been kicked around by local peasants who did not want the "dangerous strangers" to live near their villages. The migrant workers still resented being detained by state forest farm patrols for illegal logging, when the patrols knew exactly who had hired the workers to commit the offenses but were too intimidated to hold the actual culprits accountable. They also recalled illegal or poorly paid work they had undertaken out of financial need or fear of annoying their employers.

These workers spent much time and energy negotiating terms and were constantly on the move between sites and in search of fair work. This was in large part due to employers misrepresenting jobs, intentionally or otherwise. A Guizhou couple was right in the middle of this process when I interviewed them in an abandoned apartment at the state logging camp. The day before, they and their two coworkers had ridden their motorbikes four hours to get to the work site, bringing equipment, some clothes, a gas stove, and a fan. They had been told to plant small tree crops. On arrival at the site, they found that they would first need to remove old roots from the soil and then plant a type of medicinal plant that required a significant amount of tilling. Because the job was bigger than described, they refused to do it and now needed to scramble to find other work.

In spite of these difficulties, the migrants had no plans to retire soon. They could still work, and the industry still needed them. They might try to earn enough money for medical and eldercare for themselves, as well as some money for their children. It was clear, however, that they did not consider the Fujian mountains as a long-term home. They knew they would not be able to afford local housing, and their rural household registration still made it difficult to resettle. They had already remodeled and upgraded their ancestral graveyards, and some had even built new family houses in their home villages.

Once again, migrant workers who were foreign to the local environment and had no historical cultural or social relationship to the native land and forests were being used as the labor for timber production. One difference between the rural migrants of the 2010s and the those of the 1950s was that the agents of capital accumulation and the owners of the means of production were not the state but capitalists; and many of these capitalists were local peasants.

Alienation from the Forest

Studies of humans' relationship to the forests amid Chinese forestry reforms in the twenty-first century tend to either focus on the legalities of ownership, rental, and uses or discuss how the rural flight to cities has promoted forest conservation and decreased environmental degradation.[20] In writing about the shifting experiences of peasants and new rural migrants, I consider other dimensions for assessing the relationships between human communities and the forests: how far away people live from the forests, how much their households rely on the forests for subsistence, and how the forests are situated in cultures, societies, and economies.

Forest management from the 1950s to the 2010s led to a gradual alienation of people from the forests. Local peasants increasingly treated the forests as commodities and moved away from them both physically and culturally. New migrant workers uprooted from their southwestern villages became the exploitable labor in the privatized forestry economy. Trees became mere assets, whose value, in both ecological and economic terms, was measured by state regulations and the wood market.

Before the Chinese revolution, Fujian peasants had lived in the highlands for generations, and the forests had been woven into their living environment and cultural beliefs. Nevertheless, after living through the decades of Communist Party forest tenure policies and urban/rural division, these local peasants had lost not only their interest in growing trees but also their cultural and social connections with the forests. Most of them had rented out their forestland and moved to the cities in pursuit of a better material and cultural life. A small group of them became timber business owners, the new capitalists in the tree market. Their accumulation of capital was shaped not only by the market but also by state interventions such as logging quotas and PES pricing. Essential to their capital accumulation was the exploitation of new migrant workers who had little physical or cultural attachment to Fujianese forests. These workers constantly moved through the mountains, longing to return home amid income, housing, and care insecurities.

During the 1950s and 1960s, the principal strategy for the state wood economy and capital accumulation in Fujian was to create a viable mixture of labor and raw materials through the expropriation of labor, land, and trees. In the twenty-first century, the forestry industry was marked by the alienation of human communities from forested and rural land. The structural inequalities formed in the earlier period incubated the change that came in the later one.

FOUR

DISPOSABLE OFFCUTS

When I first started interviewing the Shaowu sawmill workers in 2008, I consulted nineteen laid-off middle-aged workers in four cities as they looked for work nationwide. By 2013, many women were reaching retirement age and had returned to Shaowu to live in their former work-unit housing. The sawmill had built these apartments in 1970s and 1980s for workers and their families. In the early 1990s, the mill sold the apartments to the residents at a very low price as a form of employee housing benefit. Since I was alone, staying in a sawmill apartment, a group of about ten started inviting me to dinner. They frequently gathered to make dumplings and buns together; on another occasion, one woman tried a long-unused recipe for sheep's head soup. They'd known each other for decades. After the 2000 layoffs, they had scattered, temporarily lost connection, and lived dramatically divergent lives. In the 2010s, they reconnected, and the conversation at dinner featured updates on their families or former colleagues and neighbors at the sawmill.

One evening, they mentioned the health problems of a colleague named Lina:

"Lina has uremia? How shocking! How old is she?"

"She was born in 1961, same as me. We were in the same class at school. I heard about her illness at our junior high school reunion a few days ago."

"What a pity! We were never close. But I remember she was always very talented and artistic."

After that, people shared their memories about Lina: a woman from a cadre's family, she was gifted at painting, singing, and photography—yet aloof, unlikable, and odd. They worried about her. Because she was unmarried and childless, they feared there was nobody to take care of her except her elderly mother. I listened quietly, not knowing that in a few months, Lina and I would have many deep conversations about life and death, about living with a sense of injustice, and about her community as the disposable labor for Chinese economic development.

By the end of the Mao era, the state forestry workers' communities had developed a sense of ownership over the land, the facilities, and the wood products of the industry. Although they could not commodify these materials without the state's permission, they were entitled to employment, infrastructure, welfare, and family and community togetherness, and they could occasionally use wood for their personal or household needs (for example, using wood offcuts as fuel). This was how Chinese workers experienced the socialist rhetoric that "the people are the owners of the nation" and "the working class leads the country." However, with the capitalist transition that began in the late 1970s, the state took away the workers' sense of ownership of the state industry and means of production (land, factory facilities, and raw materials). They became cheap labor exploitable by the capitalist economy.

Lina, like most of the second-generation workers at the Shaowu Sawmill, was a child of workers who had been separated from their land in the northern plains in the 1950s. Her life story, interwoven with the post-Mao history of capital accumulation in the state wood-processing industry, illustrates a second round of expropriation in this industry, as well as the oppression experienced by the second generation of women workers. As a member of the state enterprise, Lina was entitled to housing, health care, education, security of employment, and other forms of social support. However, she was never officially registered as a state worker. In 1980, she and five hundred daughters of the first-generation workers were recruited to work in the sawmill. The sawmill called these young women "surplus laborers" and registered them as "collective workers," a feminized, second-class employment status. Like their mothers (classified as dependent workers), these women were supposed to feel thankful for the employment opportunities offered by the benevolent state. When the state sawmill began privatization, women were laid off earlier, compensated with much lower severance pay, and given much smaller pensions because the sawmill had not treated them as state workers and therefore had not paid into their social security funds. Lina's acute sensitivity to injustice and her criticism of the Chinese state's treatment of workers—especially women—inspired much of my analysis in this chapter.[1]

Daughters and Offcuts

Lina's parents were both from Shandong. Her father was a high-ranking military veteran, and her mother grew up in an affluent family and received a private school education. They had a dramatic wedding ceremony in the 1950s in which her father rode a horse to pick up her mother. Her father came to Fujian in 1958 shortly after their wedding, and her mother followed him a couple of years later. They lived in a city in central Fujian until they were caught in the factional battles of the Cultural Revolution. By then her father was the city police chief, and his powerful position and class privilege made him a target. Their home was broken into, and both parents were violently hit with metal objects in a bloody scene that formed one of Lina's most striking childhood memories. Six months later, her father managed to get a transfer to the relatively calm Shaowu. He became the Shaowu sawmill security department's manager, and her mother taught at the mill-run school and was a propaganda performer.

Lina and her brothers joined their mother in the school's propaganda performance team, and each of them played multiple roles in the choir, instrumental ensemble, and dance group. They also belonged to the Chinese calligraphy and painting team. Ten-year-old Lina developed two hobbies that would later draw her out of sawmill life: mountain hiking and stage makeup. She loved to travel to the Shaowu villages to perform for the peasants, mainly because of the hours of hiking through mountains and fields. She did the makeup for herself and other child performers, and her skills surpassed those of the adults on the team.

The propaganda team stopped touring the villages after the end of the Cultural Revolution in 1976, and Lina, a junior high graduate, started an informal employment at the sawmill. Adolescent children of state workers worked on demand in the family dependent production team alongside their mothers, but their hours were even more irregular. Lina worked five to ten days a month. Since her earnings and rationed food were insufficient to support her, she mostly relied on her parents. Like many other mill families, Lina's parents, despite their comparative privileges, were very anxious about their children's employment prospects at the end of the 1970s.

During the Cultural Revolution, at least one or two youths from each sawmill family were sent to rural areas to "undergo reeducation by poor peasants."[2] When they gradually returned to urban Shaowu, starting in 1977, unemployment was widespread. At the same time, as China's capitalist economic transition began, the central government ordered many state-run factories (including the sawmill) to limit labor costs by reducing hiring. At that time, hiring at the sawmill followed the replacement (*buyuan*) recruitment model.[3] Based on quotas set by the central and provincial governments, the sawmill guaranteed a job to just one child of each retiring state employee. Most state workers let one of their sons use this quota. Some families sent their sons to the military for two years, which would ensure employment on their return. That is why many daughters of the first-generation sawmill workers were working in the family dependent production team at the end of the 1970s, anxiously hoping for stable employment.

The state-enterprise-affiliated collective enterprise (*guoying dai jiti*) that emerged to remedy women's unemployment at this time was a variation on urban collective enterprises, which reappeared after a pause during the Cultural Revolution. An urban collective enterprise, a transitional form between private and state ownership of the means of production, was usually "created and managed by cities, counties, towns, and urban neighborhoods" to hire unemployed urban residents, especially women.[4]

Despite the general directive limiting new hires, the Fujian provincial government allowed the state enterprises to establish collective enterprises based on their existing family dependent production team, using the vague word *capacity* to allow scope for local negotiations and variations. Because no state logging camp in Shaowu started a collective enterprise, the women workers received no pension at all (a situation that led to a ten-year-long protest that I describe in chapter 6). Fortunately, the head of the sawmill's family dependent production team, Yongchun Wu, worked hard to turn the team into a collective enterprise. Because her husband was the head of Shaowu Sawmill, she had access to critical information and networks. She repeatedly visited the provincial and county governments to facilitate the administrative process. The assets that the team had already accumulated from the 10 percent withheld from salaries (not all of which needed to be spent on clothes and equipment) gave her some leverage. "Our team had saved one million yuan at that time!" many dependent workers told me (which was a bit of an exaggeration). The state sawmill provided funding, machines, and administrative support. Given the disproportionate rate of unemployment among women and the state economy's focus on cutting labor costs, the sawmill-affiliated collective enterprise was the best available compromise, born of the different needs of the state, enterprise, cadres, and workers.

The collective enterprise turned first-generation family dependents into officially registered collective workers and recruited their unemployed daughters as well. When it started in 1980, 95 percent of the five hundred collective workers were female. The sawmill's official announcement of the establishment of the collective enterprise explained that it would use the "surplus laborers" (the state workers' unemployed daughters) as well as the "wood offcuts" from the state enterprise's production line. By equating these workers' labor with waste materials from factory production, the state could claim legitimacy—and even benevolence—in exploiting both.

Lina was pleased about the establishment of a collective enterprises. People still strongly adhered to the Maoist ideology that contributing to the state and society through paid work was necessary in order to lead a meaningful life. The sawmill leaders declared in a public meeting that the collective workers would be rewarded in the same manner as their state counterparts. Soon, however, Lina realized that the wage scales for collective workers were lower than those for the state workers. The difference was not great: for example, an entry-level state worker earned ¥31, while a collective worker earned ¥28. What bothered her more was the unequal treatment collective workers experienced on the shop floor and in their daily interactions with state workers.

The collective's workshop was much smaller than the state enterprise workshops, so some collective workers were seconded to work at the state workshops temporarily. Even though they were doing the same duties as their state worker colleagues, they were paid at the lower rate of collective employees.

When Lina started as a collective worker, she did one of the least popular tasks at the state particleboard workshop: cleaning the wire mesh and iron board that compressed the wood fibers into a mat. She used a blowtorch and a metal brush to remove fibers stuck to the board and mesh. She worked with her face in a constant blast of hot air, scrubbing stubborn spots and moving the fifty-kilogram board with her own thirty-eight kilogram body. Lina and another collective worker took turns working the graveyard shift (11 p.m. to 7 a.m.), while the state workers took only the day or swing shifts.

What made Lina angriest was not the pay disparity but the way collective workers were treated like "second-class citizens." The manager berated the collective workers for being late to work, but not the state workers. The state workers also often belittled them with phrases like "You are merely a collective worker." Once Lina brought an apple to eat at work and got a scolding from her supervisor. She pointed out that the other day a state worker had brought snacks to work, but the supervisor hadn't said anything. After a few similar conflicts, Lina quit the state workshop.

> My dad said I was a "thorn." I think he was right. Many collective workers were bullied but didn't make a peep. They probably internalized the discrimination and so could tolerate the inequality. But I couldn't. I was so angry. I stayed at home for half a year and did not like to have any interactions with state workers after that. I didn't have any income and just relied on my dad's salary. Although my dad criticized me for being a thorn, he was supportive of me. He did not push me to work and just let me rest at home. After quite a while, he went to talk with the sawmill managers and found a new position for me.

"Thorn" (*citou*) is a northern Chinese epithet for an antisocial and head-strong person. Lina further attracted the label with her lack of interest in matchmaking and marriage. The marriage market at the sawmill was hierarchical. Two state workers marrying was seen as the most admirable type of match; a male state worker marrying a female collective worker was ordinary and fine. The male collective workers, ranking lowest in the hierarchy, usually married women from outside the sawmill. Marriage between state and collective workers was a crucial reason why the collective workers tolerated their lower salaries: the state worker's higher income was seen as a shared family wage.

Housing was scarce in urban China. When employees married and left their parents' homes, they could apply for an apartment through their work unit. This was one reason why sawmill workers mostly married young. Since state workers had priority in the allocation of housing, young female collective workers were eager to marry their state worker colleagues. Matchmaking by senior supervisors and colleagues was common. Lina, who had no patience for the hierarchy or the inequity and no interest in dating state workers, frequently rejected people's well-intentioned matchmaking. Soon she became known as aloof and arrogant.

From Corporatization to Clear-Cutting

In the Mao era, the work units served as means of organizing the labor force to develop the national economy, maintaining urban residents' livelihoods, and instilling in workers the party-endorsed progressive ideology. In the post-Mao era, state enterprises were transformed into corporations prioritizing productivity and competition. Following Deng Xiaoping's call for exploratory reforms, "crossing the river by feeling the stones," many of these enterprises restructured repeatedly between 1980 and 2000, altering labor relations, labor organizations, and the laborers' perception of their work. Downsizing state enterprises and instead establishing collective enterprises was one of the early approaches.

In the Mao era, state enterprises had to submit all net income to the government. In the post-Mao era, state enterprises reformed their incentive plans. In the early 1990s, the Shaowu Sawmill started running its various workshops as separate companies through the establishment of "production responsibility systems." At the beginning of each year, the sawmill manager asked workshop managers to make sales and production plans. At year's end, if the workshops exceeded these goals, they could keep the surplus income.

In the Mao era, state workers received a stable monthly income, and dependent workers were compensated based on days worked and assignments completed. This gendering of labor organization and payment made female workers rely on their self-discipline much more than their male counterparts did. In the post-Mao era, this incentive mechanism extended to men as well. What had started in the 1980s as a program of stable monthly salaries plus outcome-based bonuses for both state and collective workers became merely piece wages in the 1990s. Workers had less security and, more importantly, they consciously linked their individual productivity to their individual compensation.

When asked about how the performance-based compensation system influenced workers' productivity, a sawmill worker named Bao Yixiong answered: "We had worked hard and whole-heartedly until our compensation started being based on our work performance. When workers were not mainly concerned about the money, we cared about our work quality. But when everyone else was only working for more money, we too only worked when it led to money. That was the time people started being lazy and trying to work less."

Bao's statement challenged the post-Mao capitalist dogma that performance-based compensation always promotes higher productivity and that all workers were inefficient in Maoist China. He pointed out in his interview with me that other, nonmaterial incentives could motivate hard work—for example, being a member of a collective, feeling proud of the worker identity, and experiencing the satisfaction of contributing to a collective cause (for example, socialist modernization). When the evaluation of productivity and the method of disciplining laborers became individualized, individual productivity might grow, but resistance to that discipline might grow as well—including finding ways to work only when it really counted. In this way, introducing performance-based evaluation could be counterproductive.

Starting in the mid-1990s, another cost-cutting measure was implemented to "get rid of the burdens of state enterprises." The "burdens" were the state enterprises' provision of social welfare and services to the workers. Financial responsibility for children's education, utilities, neighborhood services, social security, and medical care was gradually shifted from work units to private firms or individuals, with the government paying a portion. With the simultaneous increase of private businesses, the decline of central planning, and the abolition of the rationing system, the work unit was no longer the nucleus of urban life.[5]

Meanwhile, the state enterprises began exploring ways to sell labor to generate revenue. In the 1990s, the sawmill's collective enterprise hired out some of its workers to other enterprises. Lina and several coworkers were sent to work at a local bank. The bank paid the mill for the labor, and the mill compensated the workers after deducting a percentage. Essentially, the sawmill served as a human resource agency that provided services to other work units. Lina hated the bank job. She resented the bank employees, who earned much more than the transferred sawmill employees, and sometimes she openly rejected assigned tasks.

Finally, she found an opportunity to escape that work. A businessman started a photography studio near the bank. On opening day, he recruited ten female models for a demonstration of portrait photography. Lina, who had excelled at makeup since she was a ten-year-old in the propaganda performance team, was hired to do makeup for these models. Her work impressed the businessman, who later hired her for other projects. Soon, this part-time job interfered with her job at the bank, and once she skipped a bank shift to work at the studio. Her older brother, notified by her bank supervisor, ran into the studio to take her away and scold her. "You have a formal job, and now, you are working for this private business?" Employment at a private business was considered unstable and thus despised.

What Lina's older brother, a male state worker, could not understand was that Lina, as a second-class employee at the sawmill and the bank, had not been treated as someone with a "formal job" for a very long time. Lina recalled that moment: "I always respected my older brother and usually followed his advice. But that time, I did not listen to him. I didn't say anything, but I did not leave the studio. I earned a much higher hourly pay at the studio, and the boss respected me a lot because of my proven skills. At the bank, I wasn't treated as an equal."

In the mid-1990s, the sawmill developed another way to cut labor costs: it started encouraging employees to take early retirement or unpaid leave. Early retirement was open only to workers who were less than five years away from the statutory retirement age. The sawmill paid them a fraction of their former wage (without any bonus) until they became eligible for a state pension. Between the mid- and late 1990s, about 5 percent of the sawmill workers took early retirement or unpaid leave. The majority were collective workers. In most situations, they chose this option because they could earn more in private businesses than as collective workers, or because they were tired of the unequal treatment in the sawmill. But giving up a stable job in a state industry was still generally a controversial move. Lina took unpaid leave in 1997 and started working at the studio full-time.

The sawmill started yet another reform project in 1998. In a variation on a common nationwide practice, it tried to transform the collective enterprise into a joint-stock company by requesting that every employee buy a minimum of ¥3,000 in stock. Even though Lina no longer worked there, she paid the money in order to maintain her labor relationship with the sawmill. Ideologically, she valued the collective worker identity, and she also wanted the implied guarantee of permanent employment. Like almost all state and collective workers at that time, she believed in the state's promise to protect the workers and the legitimacy of government-led reforms.

This nationwide experiment could have been a path toward creating employee-owned cooperative enterprises, but it ended up being merely a way to "borrow" money from the workers, who could not refuse this request. After the collective workers put in their stock money, they were still not involved in any decision-making. The money was later returned to the workers when the collective enterprise was fully privatized at the turn of the century.

The restructuring measures of the 1980s and '90s had the effect of distancing workers economically, ideologically, and physically from their roles as "owners" of the state enterprises. A subsequent measure would completely strip the workers of their ownership, along with their entitlement to those enterprises' assets and resources.

By the end of the 1990s, the idea that state enterprises were inefficient and state workers were lazy had become widely accepted. Party newspapers and leaders explicitly criticized state workers and state enterprises for wasting national resources and weakening the national economy. One famous saying at the time was that state workers were "eating rice from the big pot" of state enterprises, and state enterprises were "eating rice from the big pot" of the national economy. At the same time, it seemed evident that central planning and the state enterprises' monopoly over some market sectors hampered productivity. That was also the time when China was making the final push to join the World Trade Organization (WTO). By then, the Chinese central government was attempting to popularize the idea that "linking up with the world" would eventually energize the Chinese economy. In order for China to succeed in a global economy ruled by the capitalist free market and competition, the unproductive and costly state workers needed to be replaced with a more qualified labor force.

These two interrelating discourses legitimized both nationwide privatization and worker layoffs. The popular narratives called this full-scale privatization "clear-cutting" (*yi dao qie*). By 2001, 86 percent of all state enterprises had been partially or fully privatized. Between 1998 and 2005, the number of state enterprises fell from 64,737 to 27,477.[6] The privatization caused mass unemployment in the late 1990s: between 1998 and 2001, 25.5 million workers were laid off.[7]

There were two widespread consequences of this nationwide privatization. First, it marked the final realization of the state's continuous attempts to shed the burden of providing for workers' social, medical, and educational needs, as well as footing the bill for the entire infrastructure of the workers' living environment. Whether in ideology or in practice, the owners of factories became capitalists, and the workers' only connection to their workplace was their individualized, quantifiable work performance. The workers were no longer the collective owners or the leaders of the nation or the national economy.

Second, a small group of government officials and businesspeople gained a large amount of capital by embezzling previously state-owned assets and undercompensating the laid-off workers. How else, the reasoning went, could a socialist economic system quickly transform into a capitalist one? How else could the capitalist mode of production drastically expand within an existing socialist planned economy? How else could the means of production owned by capitalists and corporations dramatically increase within a short amount of time? The Chinese state jump-started these processes by simply allowing the transfer of its capital to the new capitalist class through embezzlement and undercompensation.

Along with economic competitiveness, an equally important rationale for privatizing the wood products industry was the global concern over deforestation. The Chinese government asserted that the state monopoly on wood processing, including the price controls, encouraged inefficiency and waste. They argued that privatization and competition would force the reorganized factories to reduce wood harvesting and pursue more efficient production through advances in industrial technology and better uses of scrap wood and waste.

At the Shaowu Sawmill, the collective enterprise was privatized in 1999 and the state enterprise in 2002. The mill was divided and sold to four private businesses—one based in Shaowu, the rest in other southern provinces. These four new privately owned mills continued using the state sawmill's buildings, its energy-generation plants with their two giant chimneys, and six gantry cranes, but they put in new machinery imported from Japan and Germany that was considered more efficient.

All the sawmill workers, including Lina and her brothers, were laid off. Their relationship with the sawmill was terminated, and they permanently lost all state benefit entitlements. The severance pay they received was tied to seniority; on average, state workers (like Lina's brothers) received around ¥25,000, while the collective workers (like Lina) got ¥3,500 plus a return of the ¥3,000 they had been asked to contribute in 1998. On average, men's severance pay was six times higher than women's. Nationwide, women constituted 62.8 percent of laid-off workers.[8] Middle-aged and older women in manufacturing, in particular, were much more likely to lose their jobs.[9]

Laid-off workers in general had a terrible time finding decent jobs. Their schooling had been dramatically interrupted by the Cultural Revolution, which had resulted in many being "sent down" to the countryside. Lina and her brothers had only a middle school education. After being laid off, they entered a competitive job market that valued educational attainment.[10] Other competition came from much cheaper rural migrant workers. Because sawmill workers around the country were laid off around the same time—in many cases, like Lina's, entire extended families and communities at once—few people could rely on their social networks for job hunting.

The government's reemployment aid centers did not offer laid-off workers practical assistance in finding stable jobs; instead, their main agenda was to instill in workers the principle of "self-reliance."[11]

Middle-aged women who had been laid off found themselves in a particularly hostile job market. Job discrimination against women had proliferated in various sectors in the 1980s.[12] China's fast-developing service industry prioritized "youth occupations," which demanded physical attractiveness and mostly hired young women.[13] Many laid-off female sawmill workers found that restaurants and hotels were willing to hire them only as kitchen help and cleaners rather than waitresses and front-desk receptionists, because middle-aged women were considered "too old" for positions that involved interacting with the customers.

The gendered reemployment of the Shaowu Sawmill workers aligned with the national trend but also had distinctive characteristics. The county government sold the sawmill to the four private businesses with a vague proviso that they should prioritize hiring the sawmill's laid-off state workers, but the arrangement did not take account of the collective workers, and it did not set rehiring quotas or impose any penalty for failure. So implementation mostly relied on the new owners' goodwill. Only 27.5 percent of the laid-off workers were reemployed, more men than women.[14]

Being hired back to one of the four mills was considered the best reemployment track because the workers usually had contracts, stable working hours, and decent wages. However, the working hours might be much longer than at the previous state sawmill and even longer than legally allowed, and the workload could be heavy. Two of the mills paid workers social security and medical care. The other reemployment options often had no job security, regular payment, or benefits.

Lina's two sisters-in-law switched between various temporary jobs, such as cleaning at hotels and restaurants, manual work in small manufacturing workshops, and domestic help. Lina's brothers were not hired back by the four mills either. Fortunately, they had learned to play musical instruments in the propaganda performance team and formed a funeral band with a few laid-off workers from other privatized enterprises. The band played drums, bass guitar, keyboard, saxophone, and *erhu* (a two-stringed bowed instrument) at the front of the funeral procession. Lina recalled, "They didn't earn much: playing at one funeral could earn only ¥10 to ¥20. Also, they needed to pay close attention to families whose relatives were dying. Whenever they heard that a person passed away, they waited outside the apartment. Sometimes, two bands waited outside one apartment, fighting for business. It was funny and pathetic. Later, my older brother taught himself belly dance, and this big man became a belly dance trainer. I think he is the only male belly dance trainer in Shaowu." She laughed.

Even though Lina stopped working at the sawmill in 1997 and had always kept her distance from other sawmill workers, she felt strong compassion for the laid-off workers and sadness for the sawmill community. Her father had passed away, and Lina lived with her mother in the sawmill apartment. Every day when she walked through the apartment complex, she could "practically see the clouds of sorrow and worry hovering over the community." She overheard middle-aged parents apologizing to their young children for not being able to afford snacks or notebooks.

Lina had by then taken over the photography studio and was working as the boss, photographer, and makeup stylist. She had only one or two assistants. Her financial situation was good, but she had to work hard. After leaving her job at the bank, Lina had resumed an old hobby: backcountry hiking and camping. It became an escape from her anger and sadness. When she described the exhaustion of managing the photography studio as well as her family members' and neighbors' struggles, Lina looked sad and spoke poignantly. But when she told her hiking stories, her whole body was suddenly invigorated, her eyes bright and smiling, her voice loud and clear.

Starting in the late 1990s, stories about laid-off middle-aged women proliferated on television and in the press. The typical storyline featured a woman suffering in the job market because of a lack of skills, training, and flexibility, but eventually adopting the spirit of capitalism—self-reliance in the market economy and economically rational behaviors—and becoming a successful entrepreneur.[15] This discourse featuring "reemployment stars" promoted neoliberal economics and ideology.

Was Lina, a former collective worker and now a business owner and an outdoor enthusiast, a reemployment star?

In 2006, the Chinese stock market started rising rapidly, though it was still the purview of a wealthy few. But in 2007 many ordinary people began to invest their savings, including laid-off workers who had no idea what stocks were but had no other way to make money. They thought that stocks would keep climbing as long as the Chinese GDP increased, and that they couldn't possibly lose value until after the 2008 Beijing Olympic Games. The Shanghai Composite rose to a peak of 6,092 in October 2007. Lina considered investing in the stock market too risky until a bank salesperson told her that mutual funds were different from stock, and they would never drop. Lina put her savings into a mutual fund.

With the global financial crash of 2008, the Shanghai Composite dropped from above 6000 to below 2000, wiping out trillions of yuan in market value and hundreds of millions of ordinary Chinese people's savings, including those of many laid-off sawmill workers. Mutual funds, of course, dropped as well. Perhaps the salespeople deliberately lied, or maybe they didn't know what they were talking about. After all, they were not professionally trained in finance, and their job was to persuade others who knew even less than they did. Lina lost most of her savings.

At the end of 2009, rent on the studio was due to double, and Lina didn't have the funds to upgrade the photography business to meet the rent increase. She had to close her business and start working as a waitress at a small restaurant:

> I was diagnosed with diabetes. Perhaps those years of backcountry hiking and camping exhausted my body. I stopped the photography business in 2009, partly because of my health problem. After that, I stayed at home without any income. My friend introduced me to this waitressing job. He knew that I cared about saving face, so he didn't say he had found a job for me. Instead, he said: "My friend's restaurant needs someone to help them. Can you go help them out?" The salary was eight hundred per month, and with this money I could pay for my medicine, social security, and medical insurance. I thought I just needed to sustain myself for another two years until I could receive the state pension.

In the reemployment-star discourse, Lina could be seen as responsible for her own failure and for making economically irrational decisions. But the government played a role by encouraging ordinary Chinese people to invest in the newly developed financial market, knowing that most lacked any knowledge or experience and declining to offer financial literacy education. It seems predictable that these people would not be able to make "economically rational" decisions. Within this irony, the stock crisis seemed not surprising but inevitable.[16]

Discarded Laborers

The 2000 enterprise privatization "freed" a whole class of state workers from their collective means of production and transferred ownership of these means of production to a new class of capitalists. However, this structural formation of class divides was mostly disguised by party-endorsed narratives that portrayed the privatization and layoffs as a crisis affecting individuals and households, one that could also be solved by individuals and families. The "reemployment stars" propaganda promoted the idea of meritocracy. Another narrative constructed the "crisis of masculinity." When laid-off male workers encountered challenges in their post-layoff lives, their experiences were described as due to frustration over failing to provide for their families.[17] Many laid-off workers, both men and women, internalized this ideology and believed that the solution was to "catch up with the reforms" and adapt to the new capitalist labor market.

The following conversation over a family dinner in 2013 exemplifies this kind of internalization of state propaganda. A male former state worker, newly hired by a private factory, complained that his salary had not been paid in two months, that he was not going to receive social security or medical insurance, and that the working environment was dirty. He said he did not want to work there anymore. His sister was shocked: "You want to change work again? You just changed your job two months ago. You didn't like your previous jobs either. Can't you wait? If you quit now, you will not get your salary back." His wife added: "Right! Now, every job is like this. Where can you find a job that pays your social security and medical insurance? You are not working for a state enterprise anymore! If you don't want this one and don't want that one either, how can you find a job?"

His wife was on target: most factories now mistreated their workers. The dominant discourse in post-Mao China portrays reform as a progressive, linear development: the state economy had made massive progress, and people were expected to catch up with this progress by adapting to the changes, including the violations of labor rights. Otherwise, they would be left out, and deservedly so. At that time, the disgruntled worker's wife was working for a chemical factory. Even though she was scared in the toxic and dangerous working environment, she felt she couldn't complain, because she needed her wages. She then applied her own standards to her husband's situation.

The status of the worker fell from propaganda icon in Mao-era China to almost the underclass in the reform era. Losing your job was reframed as an individual failure instead of a class struggle, and if you couldn't embrace a capitalist entrepreneurial role, you deserved a job with terrible conditions and pay. Critical class analysis died. The state had not mismanaged change: rather, individual workers had "failed" under the myth of meritocracy.

Perhaps because Lina had always been a community outlier, she did not buy the prevailing narrative of individual failure. Instead, she attributed laid-off workers' troubles to class inequality, disposable labor, and the role of the state. "The state and society disposed of us laid-off workers to accumulate capital for some of the higher-class groups. We accumulated so much capital for the country with our hard work, and now it has all been used to feed the rich and the officials. They now ignore us. So unethical! Whenever I think about this, I feel very angry. I feel the whole society and the state owe us laid-off workers so much!" Lina's antagonism was the result of her experience of inequities through both the Mao and post-Mao eras.[18] Her comments point out that the discourses of efficiency, individualism, and meritocracy disguised the state's agenda to stop paying social welfare for employees, to tame the workers who had felt entitled to ownership of the state enterprises and a decent work environment, to render them exploitable labor, and to dispose of them. Her analysis was a worker's critique of original accumulation on the ground.

The official discourse acknowledged the dismissal of tens of millions of state workers but embellished it with a discourse of "sacrifice": the workers had sacrificed their stable jobs and lives for the country's healthy market and economic development, the implication being that they had chosen to do so. This discourse was especially pervasive in China's northeast, targeting the heavy-industry workers who were once the most honored members of

China's working class. The intertwined discourses of inefficient socialist economy and sacrifice for the nation portrayed state workers as a burden and irrelevant to the rise of China as a powerful, globalized national economy. The Chinese state had engineered the sacrifice of a group of people for national development once before: when a whole generation of rural people was surrendered for urban industrialization and modernization.

One way to dispose of laboring bodies is to make their homes invisible. When I first moved into the sawmill apartment complex in 2013, the dirtiness and darkness of the neighborhood astonished me. The state sawmill had had its own cleaning staff for the residential area; privatization ended that. The city's cleaning plan didn't cover it because it was not a public area. It was not a commercial residential complex, so there was no management company to take care of it.[19] The privatization of the sawmill cut off funding for public lighting for the whole neighborhood, including the lights in apartment hallways. So the neighborhood became utterly dark at night, except where a few families voluntarily installed lights in their apartment stairwells and paid for the electricity.

Between 2000 and 2010, Shaowu, like many other small Chinese cities, had seen growth in real estate, service and entertainment, and tourism. Streets, buildings, and public infrastructure were renovated. The Shaowu Sawmill area, however, seemed stuck in the late twentieth century. The city government ignored the mill and the associated housing in all of its urban planning projects. Like the city government, the owners of the four private wood companies invested almost nothing in revamping the factories' exteriors, the streets, or the other public spaces.

A national land-use policy in 2010 urged local governments to evict all industrial manufacturing operations from cities. The four wood companies agreed to vacate the premises and move to an industrial zone on the urban fringe after the Shaowu city government offered them 40 percent of the revenue from the sale of the land, which would become a real-estate development. The factories were demolished in 2013. At the sawmill residential area later that year, Lina and several other former sawmill workers pointed across the road to the demolished workshop buildings. Lina observed: "Soon, some new and expensive skyscraper apartments will stand across the street.... But the government never thought about making any changes for those of us who live in old apartments and live in the dirty and dark environment on the other side of the road."

In fact, when the workers first heard about the real-estate development project in 2012, they thought their residential neighborhood would be demolished and rebuilt. Some were happy, because they were tired of the messy environment and management lapses, and they thought the city government would relocate or compensate them. But others doubted that the compensation would be enough to buy a new apartment anywhere in the city.

A friend of Lina's who worked for the urban planning office told her that the planning documents for the neighborhood renewal had marks designating changes drawn only on the working area of the sawmill: the residential area on the other side of the road was blacked out and had been ignored throughout the discussion. Lina summed up the situation: "They can't see us, even though there are so many of us living here!"

It is easy to speculate about the reasons for this oversight. It was much easier for the municipal government to discuss the factory demolition with the owners of the four privatized mills and bargain over the division of revenue than to compensate two thousand residents for the loss of their homes. Housing costs were extremely high, and many of the residents were poor laid-off and retired workers, so they could be expected to drive a hard bargain with the government. To avoid cost and hassle, the municipal government chose to simply ignore this residential community in its planning.

Being overlooked by the government troubled the laid-off workers more than anything else. The city and forestry department officials never visited them after privatization, even when summer floods damaged their neighborhood. The workers also missed the cooking oil they had regularly received on holidays. In the 1960s and 1970s, cooking oil was always in short supply, so it was a meaningful benefit that enabled workers to cook nice holiday meals. In the twenty-first century, even the poorest laid-off workers could afford to buy cooking oil, so at that point the free oil became more of a symbol of the state's acknowledgement of their existence and their previous contributions. The benefit was abolished with the privatization of the sawmill.

Demolishing the factory buildings, the symbol of state industry and labor history, severed the last link between these former state workers and the means of production. It also put an end to lingering expectations that the state should be responsible for their livelihood and should "remember" their sacrifice and their contribution to capital accumulation. Now that the factories were dismantled, the residential area might lose its meaning as workers' housing and become simply a dark, dirty ghetto. What the state did not anticipate was that these laborers' feelings of abandonment, betrayal, and neglect would contribute to their collective actions starting in 2014.

FIVE

SPEAKING BITTERNESS

"Old Miao, the reporter wants to interview you." The *nainai* ushering me into the residential community of retired logging camp workers pointed to me. The old man she was talking to had his white shirtsleeves and grey pants rolled up, and he sat on a flight of steps with his back straight. Beneath grey knitted brows, a pair of cautious eyes looked at me. I was trying to use my camera to capture the scene of the old workers sitting on and around the steps of the courtyard, chatting or playing cards. But suddenly I felt embarrassed at the old man's alert eyes staring at me and my camera. Hearing the grandma introduce me as a reporter made it worse, especially since I had repeated to her many times that I was not a reporter. But I was a young person with a professional camera asking for an interview — what else could I be?

I introduced myself, using my student identity and family connection to legitimize my presence. "Hello, Miao *yeye* [grandpa], my family name is Zhou. I'm a doctoral student. I'm writing my dissertation, and I wonder if you can tell me about your work and life in the logging camp. My family members worked for the Shaowu Sawmill, so I'm writing about the history of the state forestry workers." After asking some questions about my family and my interviews with other forestry workers, he seemed less doubtful and started talking about the logging camps. Surprisingly, instead of focusing on his own experience, he told me how the state "fooled" the women dependent workers into coming to Fujian to work in the logging camps in the early 1960s. He mentioned how, for decades, the local government and the logging camps had illegally ignored the dependent workers' rights to employment benefits. He quoted directly from legal provisions, citing the years that these legal articles and acts were released, to prove that the government had acted illegally. He vividly described how he negotiated with and bested the cadres with his legal knowledge, seemingly unconcerned that I was filming his criticism of the government. At some moments, I felt that he was performing: were the other workers, my camera, and I his audience? Or maybe he was trying to use the interview as an opportunity to let his former coworkers know about his contribution to their protest against the government? I could not figure it out, but his speech, as well as my camera, attracted much attention from other elders. They looked at us, discussed the scene we had created, came closer to listen, and even jumped into the conversation.

Another *nainai*, holding her wooden knitting needles and a half-completed sweater, walked up to him and whispered: "Did you tell her about our situation?" Even though Miao said, "Yes, I'm telling her about the issue now, and don't hurry—we need to tell it step by step," she seemed anxious and decided to offer her own account. "We worked for the logging camp for thirty years. We came when we were still girls. At that time, we wore ragged clothes and worked in the mountains no matter whether the days were rainy or dark. Our jobs were so bitter (*ku*), but now they don't give us our pensions."[1] When she talked to me, her sharp eyes and upturned mouth and the waving needles in her hands all made me feel she was antagonistic. "You must write about us, and let those central [government] leaders know. You must." She turned to another old woman and said to her, "We need to push her to write about us, no matter whether it will be useful or not." Her participation in the interview attracted more men and women to join the conversation, which gradually developed into an interesting symphony: Old Miao and two other men slowly listed the legal problems, while *nainai*s interjected remarks from time to time, highlighting the bitterness of their previous work at the logging camps and urging me to report their issues. "Youngster, don't you think our lives are bitter? You must write about us."

The year was 2014. These elders were among a group of a thousand retired state logging camp workers, women and men, who had begun protesting and petitioning the government in 1998 to solve a labor rights issue that affected women dependent workers. I was impressed by how fluently the men recited the legal provisions, and I was even more affected by words of the women. The way they talked about the bitterness in their lives was familiar to me from my life history interviews with the elder women forestry workers. What's more, my maternal grandmother had used the term when she talked over and over about the adversities in her life, always with the same examples. Periodically, she asked rhetorically: "Oh, is my story bitter? Is your grandma's story bitter? It's bitter. I have been bitter my whole life."

"Speaking Bitterness" in Maoist Campaigns

The invocation of bitterness derives from the terminology of a Mao-era state governance tool that these women appropriated to serve their own needs. *Bitter* in Chinese can refer to a bitter taste in the mouth, the condition of hardship and suffering (a usage that originates in Buddhist texts), or the feeling of misery. "Speaking bitterness" (*suku*) was a traditional oral genre in Chinese rural society, often used by old women talking to other villagers about their difficulties in the domestic domain. It was co-opted by the Chinese Communist Party in a series of political campaigns, starting with the Land Reform Campaign (1950–53). Party officials and activists held group meetings where role models spoke about their prerevolutionary experiences of oppression and exploitation and praised the changes that Communist reform had brought (or might bring) to them. These speakers, typically women and elderly peasants, were called "protagonists of bitterness" (*kuzhu*). The narrative form of speaking bitterness—denouncing past sufferings and celebrating the happiness of the present—created a universal, oversimplified experience of overcoming oppression. These performative speeches, which served as models for the listeners, narrowed the gap between the Communists' newly constructed class discourse and rural residents' real lives.

Most of the land in northern China was owned not by landlords, as the party claimed, but by middle peasants.[2] The opposition between landlords (cast as oppressors who owned all the means of production) and the peasants (the oppressed who did not own any means of production) was a construct of the Communist narrative that did not match the reality.

Many landowners in fact had good relationships with their tenants and hired laborers, and peasants were often reluctant to condemn them.[3] In the speaking-bitterness meetings, people from the "exploited" classes were urged to identify, shame, and violently treat those who had "exploited" them and sometimes, according to historian Philip Huang, "manufacture class enemies even where none objectively existed."[4] This institutionalized narrative taught rural people to identify within the state-defined class divisions, to rework their personal sufferings into a narrative of state-endorsed class struggle, and to conceptualize their own lives with ideological terms like *landlord, exploitation,* and *class.*[5] Speaking bitterness was a means for the newly founded state to legitimize land collectivization and expropriation.

Speaking-bitterness meetings were used in urban Communist political campaigns as well, although these usually were not as violent and divisive as the rural ones. In one case, workers from Shanghai visited each factory in Hangzhou to talk about the oppression all workers faced.[6] The first-generation forestry workers told me about many speaking-bitterness meetings held at the sawmill and logging camps in Shaowu, both small group sessions and whole work-unit gatherings. I found some records of these meetings in the Shaowu Sawmill official archive in 2013. One of them, from 1966, reported on the outcomes of organizing family dependent workers to study the works of Mao Zedong.[7]

The report opens with a quotation from an essay by Mao Zedong titled "Mobilize Women into Production, Solve the Problem of Insufficient Labor Power": "Chinese women are a kind of great human resource, and we must utilize this kind of resource in order to build a great socialist country."[8] Then it proudly announces that mill cadres had successfully "used Mao Zedong Thought to arm the family dependent women."[9] The report states the women had once "carried very backward thoughts, . . . been very selfish, . . . and picked only easier and higher-paid tasks to do." Studying Mao Zedong Thought, however, gave these women "an unprecedented rise in their political consciousness and therefore brought about a huge improvement in their production and organizing work." But because almost all the family dependent women workers were from the villages and illiterate, the report went on, it was challenging to organize the study sessions. This challenge triggered the use of speaking bitterness meetings:

We involved [the family dependent workers] in the practice of class struggle, to awaken their need to study Chairman Mao's works. We selected a few people who had experienced great bitterness and accumulated deep resentment in the old society. We trained them to conduct educational work through modeling remembrance and comparison—recalling the bitterness of the past and contrasting it with the sweetness in the present. An old woman from Shandong recalled her miserable sixteen years as a beggar and said: "When I hold my grandson, I think of the bitterness that I experienced in the past. When I put on the new clothes that my son bought for me, I think of the kindness of the Communist Party and Chairman Mao."

The report describes how these meetings, held throughout the mill, inspired all family dependent workers to conduct "remembrance and comparison" and learn quotations from Mao Zedong. The mill cadres were even able to use these quotes "to educate family dependents and solve interpersonal conflicts between the dependents."

Work units were organized not only to carry out specific tasks but also to develop the socialist political awareness of the labor force. Through political education, "selfish" women with "backward thoughts," haggling over pay or workload, would become productive socialist laborers who would treasure the opportunity to work. This objective was consistent with the sawmill's claim that employing women dependent workers was a benevolent move by the state to help support the male workers' families.

The rhetoric of the campaign, intended to give women with no formal education a narrative structure for their lives, was typical of efforts by the modern Chinese state to establish and maintain social order through personal transformation. By creating exemplary heroes and heroines through its awards and chosen representatives, the state encouraged individuals to connect their own past with the collective memory and culture that the state was seeking to establish. With these tactics the state could also defend the morality of its promoted culture and social order.[10]

Sometimes imitating the speaking-bitterness narrative meant that the women had to twist their stories a little, changing the wording and omitting some details or exaggerating others. After some women started speaking bitterness outside the mill's organized study sessions, the practice gradually extended to almost all women and some men in the mill. In the absence of other influences that might have come from schooling or reading, it became the primary way for these mostly illiterate workers to understand and explain their lives.

Women workers born in the 1930s and 1940s, especially those from rural areas, each told me at least one story of prerevolutionary childhood suffering filled with vivid details of cold, hunger, pain, and humiliation. I laughed with recognition at the anthropologist Lisa Rofel's comment in her book *Other Modernities* that she felt that the oldest generation of women textile workers "complained a lot" and that their narratives seemed "a bit overdone," even though Rofel was trying to provide "an empathetic audience." Not until later did Rofel realize the women were carrying out "a historically and culturally specific narrative practice"—that is, speaking bitterness. In fact, if you've ever asked a Chinese woman of that generation about her life, it would be surprising if she did not complain about the bitterness she experienced in her early life. State-sponsored speaking-bitterness meetings were hosted all over China throughout the Maoist period.

Waipo's Speaking Bitterness across Time

My maternal grandmother (*waipo*), Zhou Xinlian, learned her style of personal narrative, centering bitterness, from this and similar campaigns. The pattern was reinforced by her immersion in a cultural and political environment where many women recalled their lived experiences in the same terms. Recalling a bitter life became an essential channel through which she and other women could connect to the party-state, to socialist development, to the newly built collective, and to each other.

Below I present her narrative, which was about twenty-five minutes long. Told in chronological order, it is filled with examples of suffering. Her narrative seemed scripted to me because all the examples stayed the same, and I had heard them hundreds of times as I was growing up. Moreover, she was unwilling to go beyond this narrative even when I specifically asked her to talk about something else. No matter how I framed my questions, she replied, "I don't remember that. How can I remember that?" or "I don't know how to describe it." Then she went back to her scripted narrative: "My life was bitter (*ku*) from my childhood. We were liberated when I was sixteen, and my father died when I was ten."[11]

Her life story starts from the condition and feeling of bitterness. She was born in a Zhejiang village just north of Fujian in 1934. Her family moved to Fujian when she was four. After her father's death, she was "gifted" by her mother to the household of a landlord (*dizhu*) as a servant, as her mother couldn't afford to raise her. "My mother didn't have labor power [*laodong li*]. She had no way out. People in the old society were very bitter. . . . I couldn't labor [*laodong*] at that time either.[12] Women in the old society [*jiu shehui*] couldn't labor but merely raised pigs and did house chores. They couldn't do farming work [*zhong di*]."

She wept as she recalled living in the landlord's household from age ten to sixteen, then her escape and, shortly afterward, the "liberation" (*jiefang*) of the town by the Communist army. "I was lucky that we were liberated, so that they [the landlord's family] did not dare to take me back by force. Otherwise, they would have come! I did all the work at their house. Their daughter was the same age as me, or one year younger. They made warm clothes and shoes for her, yet they didn't even give me a single pair of shoes. When it was snowing, I was barefoot, carrying water outside."

After she ran away, she worked for another family. When she turned eighteen in 1952, she started working at a privately owned sawmill. She emphasized that there were not many women workers in the sawmill at that time, and she was paid quite well because she often worked two shifts in a row. By contrast, the landlord's family came to grief: the husband committed suicide during the Three-Antis Campaign (1951), leaving a wife who could not labor. Their daughter "had to marry a peasant and would remain a peasant through her whole life." For my grandmother, who had the privileged identity of state worker with an urban household registration, being a peasant implied that the landlord's daughter did not have a good life.

Some of the details in my grandmother's stories appear to be intentionally (and perhaps not entirely truthfully) aligned with the Chinese Communist Party discourse of the Mao era. While the CCP narrative emphasizes the exploitative rental and wage-labor relationships between landlords and renters or employees, historically, these relationships more often existed between middle and poor peasants. Middle peasants often rented a few plots of land from other middle peasants and hired poor peasants as day labor to work on that land.[13] Of the wealthier landlords who conformed to the CCP's definition, many were absentees or families whose working members had passed away.[14] So although my grandmother may have been fostered by another family for a time, being gifted by her mother to a landlord's household sounds more like party discourse than a common historical phenomenon. As for the death of the landlord, the Three-Antis Campaign was intended to stamp out corruption, waste, and bureaucracy. It mostly targeted bureaucrats, political opponents, and capitalists rather than landlords, so it is unclear how this campaign could have caused his death. My grandmother might have confused it with another campaign around the same period, such as the Land Reform Campaign.

At the core of the speaking-bitterness narrative form was the contrast between the "old society" and the "new society." Women's personal narratives could draw on different life events, class enemies, and political vocabulary to build this contrast and to align with the CCP discourse of the emancipation of women. My grandmother's version of events enabled her to highlight her exploitation by the landlord's family in the "old society" and attribute the punishment of the exploiters to the CCP in the "new society."

My grandmother's narrative also contrasted the women of the old society and the liberated women, like herself, in terms of "labor power," a term that came from Mao and official party discourse. She and her mother, who had been limited to household chores, did not have labor power until after the revolution, when women could work in the factories.

Mao Zedong's essay "Mobilize Women into Production" declares: "When women are encouraged to join the labor army, they walk out from the traditional family domain and enter into the public domain, and they should be treated as a major source of labor power." Yet the implication that Chinese women had previously stayed within the household, doing things that did not generate exchange value, was inaccurate. Poor women, particularly, worked outside the home. Additionally, women could earn money through weaving and other cottage industries. Mao's wording intentionally created a divide between the productive work that the party-state valued in its official narrative and the domestic and care work that was equally necessary, but which the party belittled in its narrative and for which it offered no support. This attitude ties in with the rhetoric that women should treasure their work opportunities at the factories and not complain about lower pay or heavier loads. Both discourses were essential to the state's extraction of women's surplus labor and the accumulation of capital.

Even though Waipo used the party-state terminology, she didn't necessarily believe implicitly in this hierarchical division of labor or consider domestic labor valueless. In fact, her narrative was full of bitterness about the work of bearing and raising children. By contrast, she shared no details of her paid work except for the title of her position and the product of her workshop. Even when I directly asked her about her coworkers, work processes, schedules, and machines, she answered: "I don't remember," "I can't describe that," or "How can I still remember that?" After withholding those answers, she went back to her preferred stories, the ones related to the trials of rearing and supporting dependent children.

Here is how she told the story of her postrevolutionary life. In 1952, she married a coworker at the sawmill where she worked. By 1964, she had given birth to four children. When the mill restructured into the state-run Shaowu Sawmill, she was registered as a state worker. Her husband died from a chronic lung disease in 1964, and a year later she was transferred into the Shaowu Sawmill, bringing along the four children. She talked little about her work or her late husband, seeming to mention them merely to introduce the stories she wanted to emphasize: her difficulty and success in raising her children and guiding them into urban state-enterprise work and marriage.

Raising four children while working full time meant, in my grandmother's stark words, "working day and night" and "having no time to take a shit." To truly launch them into adulthood, she also had to finance their weddings. Many times as I was growing up, I'd heard the story of how she raised and sold two pigs to get money for her oldest son's wedding: "At that time, I didn't even have money for him (my oldest son) to get married . . . So I raised pigs in a place by the hill. I bought two piglets that weighed eight *jin* in total. Every morning, I went to pick leaves, chopped them into pieces, and boiled them in a pot until they were very soft. I fed them to the pigs. Each pig grew to be over three hundred *jin*, and I sold both for five to six hundred yuan."

She also detailed how each child found work in a state enterprise in the late 1970s, when children of first-generation sawmill workers were massively underemployed. Her description of securing jobs for her children included twists, detours, and clever solutions. My mother, her youngest child, was born after her husband had passed away.

> When your mother was born, people told me to put her up for adoption. I was unwilling. I didn't want to. She would be bitter staying with me, but would be much more bitter being adopted by others. I funded her school study until her junior high graduation. She said she didn't want to continue, and wanted to go to the countryside as a sent-down youth instead. I told her no. A girl should not go to the countryside. Girls need to go to school. Women like me having no school education is so pathetic. But she didn't want to continue going to school. So I asked a doctor to write a fake note saying that I was too sick to continue working and applied for early retirement at age forty-seven to let my daughter take my position [at the sawmill]. Actually I could still work at that time, so after my retirement, I found another job guarding a warehouse for a factory.

After living through the Maoist ideological campaign that devalued women's domestic labor, why would my grandmother put her care work at the center of her life story narrative? This question puzzled me for a long time, until I interviewed my oldest uncle and my mom. Their recollections revealed the connection between her narrative performance, her widowhood, and her creative and necessary way of seeking support for her family.

My grandmother was an atypical state worker: not only was she a woman, but she was also illiterate and never a party activist like Zhuang Jinxian. She was able to retain the status of state worker largely because of her widowhood. Her husband had been too sick to work for quite a few years before his death, and the state recognized the need for a family to have a stable wage earner. Therefore, even during the economic downturns, when some other women state workers were laid off in the early 1960s, my grandmother kept her permanent-employee status.

As a widowed state worker, my grandmother held two different gendered roles. She was the man of the house—the sole breadwinner. Her position as a state worker not only brought in money but also entitled her four children to the benefits of the work unit: housing, education, medical care, and so on. She was also the woman of the house, the person who had to perform almost all the work for the family. This included securing jobs for her children, to which they were entitled through her status as a state worker at the mill.

My uncle and mother recalled my grandmother's sobbing about her sufferings in front of the factory cadres in order to secure employment for her children. This strategy succeeded in the state work unit, which was supposed to take care of the workers and their families. Obviously, my grandmother had mastered the speaking-bitterness technique (though she employed it to a somewhat different end), and all her children found work in three different state enterprises in Shaowu. While other (male) state workers had time to build friendships with the cadres and got help to secure jobs for their children that way, my grandmother juggled multiple shifts of work inside and outside the home. Her ability to speak bitterness to the representatives of the state: the bitterness of about the hardships of being a widow raising four children was a form of nonmaterial and affective labor that created important value for her family.

Studying postsocialist economic transitions in Poland, the geographer Elizabeth Dunn found that before privatization, workers constructed their "embedded personhood" through a kind of labor that built relations between people, not between people and things or between things and other things. By producing objects that were used by other workers, workers built human connections and situated themselves within a collective identity. This work was a significant means of generating value in socialist Poland, but its value was intrinsically not measurable through the capitalist accounting system.[15] I would categorize attending class-struggle sessions and performing speaking bitterness as a similar kind of labor.

My grandmother labored continuously, actively shaping her relationships with the cadres and thereby with the state. Through them she reminded the socialist state of its promise to care for families. Because of the suffering she had experienced, she insisted, she was precisely the kind of person the government needed to care for, even though the bitterness that she recounted was not necessarily what the state intended women to speak about.

My grandmother's speaking bitterness intersected the public and political spheres as well as the private and domestic, crossing the boundary between paid industrial and unpaid care labor. This form of rhetoric had been taught to her to serve the state's purposes, but she learned to use it to fulfill her personal and domestic needs. By politicizing her experience of domestic burdens, she forced the state to respond. Through the labor of speaking bitterness, she created a kind of value that the state could not expropriate.

Although I did not interview her until 2011, my grandmother's scripted life-history narrative ended in the 1980s, when her children all had obtained state enterprise jobs. Thus it followed the official speaking-bitterness narrative arc of recalling the suffering of the past and creating happiness in the present. But that end point was not the end of her children's stories. With the privatization of state enterprises, my grandmother's four children were all laid off.

After the sawmill was privatized, the state stopped listening to my grandmother's speaking bitterness, and her primary audience became her family members. The children who had lost their jobs had to listen to a narrative with a happy ending that sounded not only ironic, but also as if their mother were disregarding their present difficulties and relishing her own past suffering.

Privatization not only resulted in layoffs among the second-generation workers but also seemed to belie the state's promise to take care of retired workers until their death. The first-generation workers I interviewed complained that government officials had forgotten about them and never visited them to check on their condition.

As promoted by the CCP, speaking bitterness formed a link between individuals and the party-state. The state could respond to the narrative of women workers' hardships by providing a collective recognition of past suffering, official working-class status, the identity of "liberated woman," and a promise to provide for the worker and her family. The private domain could offer no such compensations. My grandmother showed the power, positive and negative, of an individual woman's speaking bitterness. The forest farm workers' protest shows what happened when a thousand women engaged in speaking bitterness together for a decade.

The Forest Farm Workers' Protest

In the Mao era, the state enterprise work units had promised workers permanent jobs and lifelong care for their families. Working in the same forestry work units with men, women felt secure, even though they were registered as family dependents, because families were taken care of. In the reform era, the state retreated from providing full-scale, lifelong worker care. In 1991, the State Council released the "Decision on Institutional Reform of the Enterprise Employees' Retirement Insurance," and the National Social Security System was introduced.[16] Under the new system employers were required to pay social security for their employees, and the employees were entitled to pensions from the state fund after retirement. The People's Republic of China Labor Law of 1995 specified levels of social security contributions and pension payments.[17]

The forest farms paid social security only for state workers, not for family dependent workers. When the state pension system started, the dependent workers did not fully understand its implications for them, and the logging camps certainly did not spell it out. So most dependent workers and state workers continued to believe they were entitled to lifelong care. For example, as dependent workers gradually retired in the 1990s, they continued going to farm-run clinics for their health care. Soon they found out that women workers in some other forestry enterprises were receiving pensions, and they were surprised. As discussed in chapter 4, the Shaowu Sawmill had started a collective enterprise in 1980 so that all dependent workers became collective workers, eligible for sawmill social security. When the dependent workers in the forest farms recognized their disadvantaged situation in the 1990s, they complained to the camp administrators, but to no avail. Once the restructuring and layoffs started in the logging camps around 2000, the workers realized that they would soon lose access to the clinic, and the farms would stop paying for residential utilities. Most of their children who were working at the forest farms would lose their jobs and thus be unable to support their aging parents.

In 1998, dependent workers from twelve forest farms and their state worker husbands, over a thousand activists in total, started protesting against the unfair benefit allocation. They petitioned, argued, held sit-ins, and finally sued the Shaowu city government and the Forestry Department. They traveled to Fuzhou, the capital of Fujian province, to petition the Fujian Forestry Bureau and delivered petitions to the Commission for Discipline Inspection of the Central Committee in Beijing. In 2008, the City of Shaowu and the Forestry Department agreed to pay all former family dependent workers ¥325 monthly, with ¥260 in cash and ¥65 deposited into their accounts in the public health-care fund so that they could be covered by public medical insurance.

Protest is a narrative performance involving group practice and long-term reiteration. Even without explicit planning or a scripted rehearsal, activists often fell into different roles over the years. During the forest farm workers' decade-long protest, they developed a gendered division of labor: male state workers posed legal arguments, while female dependent workers engaged in speaking bitterness, just as they had talked to me, a supposed "journalist who can report to the state," in 2014.

The male workers had some advantages that helped them with networking, building connections, and arguing with officials. They generally had sufficient literacy skills to read relevant documents. For example, Miao went to the local library to read back issues of newspapers, and he kept his eye on government bulletins and copied useful sections. He also carefully saved the documents that some officials gave the workers when they went to the upper-level government offices to petition. Miao asked his grandchildren to help with online research. In addition, state workers had attended more factory meetings and listened to more official speeches than had dependent workers, so they were conversant in the official language.

Laws and legal institutions—a field of contestation subject to interpretation and manipulation—are shaped and redefined constantly by citizens' acts.[18] Anthropologist Sally Engle Merry observed that when plaintiffs in the United States, especially those from working-class or lower-class backgrounds, introduced issues that were not legally significant and were dismissed by court employees, the plaintiffs either learned more legal jargon to reinforce the legitimacy of their concerns or became emotional as a form of resistance.[19] In the Shaowu workers' coordinated protests, men were the ones who learned legal jargon, while women were the ones who became "emotional."

When their arguments were repeatedly rejected by the government and the court, the male activists learned more legal language through which to press their case. The government and the court did an end run, asserting that the laws the workers referred to were either obsolete or were enacted after the period of their employment and did not apply retroactively. The workers lost the lawsuit against the Forestry Department and were unable to get any response to their petitions from any government department.

So how did they eventually succeed in securing allowances for the former dependent workers? When I asked the activists this question, they firmly and proudly answered: "Because we kept making a fuss [*nao*] for ten years!" Accumulation of time and actions led to the success of the retired workers' protest. But what exactly prompted the government to change its response? And what enabled the activists to maintain their efforts for so long? My answer to both questions is the same: women's speaking bitterness.

Speaking bitterness acted like a slow-acting poison on their opponents, gradually eroding the state's line of defense. Even though the court and government departments managed to find ways to sidestep the legal regulations that the activists cited, sympathy for their cause grew among the individual employees of the court, the Forestry Department, and the city government. These officials' skepticism toward the official response exerted pressure on their supervisors.

I interviewed the city court judge who had presided over the retired dependent workers' lawsuit against the Forestry Department. He admitted that all of the participating court employees thought the dependent workers' request for pensions and other retirement benefits was reasonable. "All these poor old dependents, they came from Shandong and other places in the 1950s and have worked here for decades. Have you heard about what their jobs were? They worked in the mountain forests, where poisonous snakes and hornets lived. The forestry work was very bitter. However, after so many years of working, they don't even have any pension after retirement now."

I noticed that the judge had adopted the terms and phrases the dependent workers used, including *bitter*. Had he listened to the dependent workers complain about their previous jobs so many times that he started repeating what he had heard, as I had done myself? He felt sorry that he could not be more helpful to them: "We also told the Forestry Department staff: 'You can't just ignore these elders. What you are doing is really not reasonable.' But we couldn't help those dependent workers any more than that. The city government was backing its own Forestry Department, and we were under the management of the city government. We couldn't fight with our boss, so we had to rule against the dependent workers. But we really did not agree with the Forestry Department and the city government."

The city government was able to save face by letting its Forestry Department win the case, but as news of the decision spread, direct criticism from city and court employees and negative comments from the public applied social pressure on the government leaders. They backed down and agreed to pay retirement benefits.

Even though neoliberalism and individualism have become dominant philosophies in post-Mao China, some traditional Chinese and Maoist moral ideas have survived. The belief that the state is responsible for people's survival is embedded in Chinese society and governance.[20] Through speaking bitterness, the women workers invoked precisely this moral consciousness and the government's obligation to take care of the elderly, the poor, and the weak. The Maoist state had set up an expectation of family support through the work-unit system. In today's China, the cultural idea that the state is responsible for caring for elders and families persists, despite increasing contestations and denials of this responsibility. Furthermore, many Chinese people, particularly those who grew up before the 1970s reforms, accept the importance of acknowledging the state workers' contribution to the economy in the 1950s and 1960s. Many influential city court and government employees were of this age group. These factors made them receptive to the older women's speaking bitterness and prompted them to alter the state representatives' decisions.

Speaking bitterness also changed the protesters' way of understanding their own laboring past. It solidified the elders' collective identification as workers who had been oppressed and exploited. Through countless retellings of the difficulties they encountered in work and life at the forest farms, they reassessed the value they created for the forest farms. When the socialist government and the neoliberal discourse of labor and value had both devalued the family dependent workers' contributions, the activists argued that their work had been significant for forestry and economic development in Maoist and post-Mao China.

Central and provincial government documents state that the primary purpose of moving family dependents from Shandong to Fujian in the early 1960s was to "stabilize the (male) workers' emotions and production." The state declared that the family dependent workers were moved there solely as a gesture of benevolence to the workers' families. The Shaowu government interpreted the documents to mean that the dependent workers should be thankful for their jobs and not expect worker status or benefits.

In their protests, the forest farms' dependent workers contended that they were mobilized to come because Fujian province and the state forestry industry needed more laborers. In the words of one family dependent worker:

> The second day, right after we arrived here, we were taken to the mountains to work. They assigned tasks to us. Each person was required to pick fifty *jin* of twigs and branches. We had to finish our tasks. . . . How can they not recognize us as workers? Now, when the Forestry Department and the logging camps log trees and sell the wood, they are cutting down and selling the fruits of our labor. We planted all these trees decades ago. Without us dependents working hard and nurturing all the trees, how could they get their current earnings? Now they are enjoying our products, but they say we were not "workers," and we don't deserve pensions. How is that possible?

I believe the crux of the matter was the gendered division of the work. The dependent workers' tasks of planting and nurturing the trees did not yield immediately profitable results. By pointing out the flaw in this official logic and arguing that their work produced long-term revenue, they represented their work as a kind of care work for the forests and valorized their labor. The repetitive narration of shared bitterness fueled the elders' energy for their long-term endeavors and reinforced their belief in the legitimacy and necessity of their collective resistance.

In speaking bitterness, the women workers deployed a tool of state propaganda to fight against the state itself. When the party-state used speaking bitterness in the rural Land Reform campaign and in the educational campaigns targeting urban women workers in the 1950s and '60s, it was meant to solidify the workers' loyalty to the party and the state and to facilitate the state projects of land expropriation and labor exploitation. The post-Mao state devalued this rhetorical tool because it no longer furthered the state's agenda. The state and many workers began dismissing speaking bitterness as futile complaining.[21]

Other types of speaking bitterness continued in post-Mao society, however, and strengthened the governance of the new capitalist state. For example, writers of "scar literature" (*shanghen wenxue*), a popular Chinese literary genre in the late 1970s and early 1980s, used speaking bitterness to illustrate the trauma and oppressions that cadres and intellectuals experienced during the Cultural Revolution (1966–76). This rhetoric legitimized the post-Mao state's newly initiated economic and political reforms. And since the end of the twentieth century, a form of tourism called "eating bitterness" (*chiku*) has taken urban middle-class people to rural areas to eat the coarse food of rural workers of the pre-reform era. Invoking the hardships of the past reinforces appreciation of the reform-era economy and consumerism.[22]

However, the forest farm dependent workers' speaking bitterness did not serve the capitalist state's discourse. When the post-Mao neoliberal discourse disparaged the state enterprises as inefficient and unproductive, the lives and skills of state workers were also deemed irrelevant and insignificant to the newly reformed economy. Female family dependent workers were the lowest of the low. Their speaking bitterness and their storytelling overall were seen as outdated and worthless.

Many dependent workers internalized this judgment. When I first moved into the Shaowu Sawmill apartments to interview workers in 2013, the neighbors all recommended that I talk to the former top supervisors, who were all men. When I asked for suggestions for female interviewees, and neighbors introduced me to Zhuang and other women state workers because they "know better about the history and know how to talk about things." And when I finally asked family dependent workers for interviews, after some informal chats, they responded with hesitation, not thinking their stories worth documenting. Of course, I found later that women like Laoniang told their stories vividly in their interviews with me.

By contrast, the logging camp dependent workers were eager to tell me their stories when I first visited their community, even though they had been marginalized just as the sawmill workers had been. Forest farm dependent workers' speaking bitterness is a radical form of opposition to the state, as it deploys a form of narrative performance that the state had initially deployed in order to expropriate women's labor and later denounced when it was adopted by the activist workers. Even though neither the content nor the rhetorical strategy of family dependent workers' speaking bitterness has been respected in post-Mao China, they were able to use it to convince the new capitalist state to listen to the workers of the socialist past.

The women's speaking bitterness succeeded in part because it was deployed in conjunction with male workers' legal arguments. Without the latter, the dependent workers' "making a fuss" would never have attracted the attention of the local government and the Forestry Department; the dependent workers would have been stigmatized as being "irrational and crazy," just as many other long-term activists in China have been discredited by the government. On the other hand, if the activists had engaged only in official legal actions against the Forestry Department, the city government and court would have upheld the original decision against them. In China today, activists cannot expect to achieve their goals by challenging a local government department solely on legal grounds. Under these circumstances, long-term speaking bitterness aroused sympathy and empathy from the court employees and government officials, who eventually swayed the institution to grant their request.

For the generation of women who lived through the entire Maoist era, speaking bitterness was their main tool for making themselves heard by the state. The younger generation of laid-off women workers—who were more active in the job market and who had internalized more of the fundamental ideological and social changes as China entered capitalism—accumulated different tools for their oppositional actions, which they deployed in the collective workers' protest that started in 2014.

SIX

ADAPTING TACTICS

Some two hundred women, former Shaowu Sawmill collective workers, gathered in front of Shaowu City Hall early on the morning of February 26, 2014, requesting an audience with the mayor to report a rights violation that had occurred during the privatization of the mill in 1998. The protesters ranged from women in their fifties, wearing stylish and colorful clothing, to older women in their eighties, walking unsteadily. To avoid blocking the road or interfering with traffic (and risking arrest), they stayed in a loose line on the sidewalk. A dozen police officers stood in front of the building, preventing them from entering.

As the workers passed around a petition for signatures (or fingerprints, as some of the older workers were illiterate), they recalled the last time their signatures had been requested — in 1998, on a severance agreement when privatization and layoffs began at the mill sixteen years earlier. According to that agreement, terminated collective workers would receive compensation from the mill ranging from ¥3,000 to ¥4,000, depending on their length of employment. Once compensated, they would have no further relationship with the mill at which they had worked for decades. The jobs were gone, and with them the right to demand compensation or other support. Zeng Nanjin, one of the protest leaders, recalled that she did not want to sign the agreement, but managers of the enterprise had threatened her husband, who was a state worker at the mill, leaving her with no choice. Yet in 2000, when the sawmill was fully privatized, along with other state enterprises, her husband lost his job anyway (though with higher severance pay). Zeng's painful acquiescence was not enough to save her husband's career.

As they passed around and signed the petition that February morning, some workers read it aloud and talked with each other. "That's right! Our collective enterprise had so many assets. We even had two plots of land, and the managers and officials have sold one of them. But we were so foolish that we never fought." The crowd became increasingly agitated and started yelling: "We want to meet the mayor!" However, they lacked the preparation and experience to synchronize their chanting. The leaders shouted, but the followers could not keep the rhythm.

The group positioned ten women in their eighties at the front of the demonstration. The leaders, who had asked me to document the rally, said: "You go to the front to film. See if they [the police] dare to touch the elders." Through my camera, I watched *nainais* talking to the young officers, explaining that they wanted to meet the mayor, pushing forward as they spoke. The young police officers, who appeared to be in their early twenties, stood still, attempting to block the workers but not wanting to risk hurting the *nainais*. Despite the dramatic social transformation in contemporary China, respect for the elderly prevails. The officers' predicament made them look awkward. Gradually, the *nainais* pushed through the police cordon, allowing the group to squeeze through the entrance to the city hall after an hour and a half of demonstrating.

Although these women had been laid off in 1998 (or retired before that), they did not begin this collective action until 2014. What accounted for such a significant lag, and what changed for them over the course of sixteen years? What kind of knowledge and toolkits did they accumulate that turned out to be useful in their campaign?

This protest had multiple, entangled roots and triggers, and the women used a variety of discourses and tactics. They discussed with me how their post-layoff experiences changed their consciousness and values and prepared them for this collective resistance.[1]

Collective Workers

When the Shaowu Sawmill was privatized between 1998 and 2000, the four private companies that purchased the buildings and assembly lines also signed fifty-year leases with the city government for rights to use the land. Starting around 2005, the Chinese central government initiated a policy called Leave the City and Enter the Industrial Zone (*tuicheng jinyuan*) in major cities, and then in smaller cities and towns, demanding that industrial factories move from urban areas into specialized industrial areas just out of town or in the country. So in 2011 and 2012, the four privately owned wood-product enterprises relocated to the new industrial zone. The city government announced its intention to sell the abandoned sawmill site to real estate developers, dividing the revenue 60:40 between the government and the leaseholders.

In late 2013 and early 2014, the former sawmill workers learned that the proposed land sale was predicted to fetch tens of billions of yuan. On January 26, 2014, a loosely organized group of former workers, men and women, blocked a main entrance of the site, demanding to meet with government officials. They claimed that even though the state was legally the sole owner of the land, the workers who had built the mill and contributed to the development of this state enterprise deserved part of the revenue from the sale. These former laborers retained a sense of belonging to and ownership of the mill and the land it stood on. It was this sense of owning the work-unit space—and the feeling of being attached to and yet separated from it—that sparked their collective actions.

When they met with two representatives from the city government, the activists talked about how the first generation workers had built the mill together and how generations of the workers' families had lived there and contributed to production. They also claimed that their demonstration was meant to "protect the state-owned land and their collective property from slipping into the hands of private owners." After listening to the activists' requests, the representatives—all kindness— promised to look into the issue and respond to them. However, the day after the demonstration, one of the activists, a middle-aged man, was arrested for "disrupting the public order" (*raoluan gonggong zhixu*). In the Maoist era, maintaining public order was ostensibly intended to protect productivity and workers' lives. In the post-Mao era, it has become a pretext for the government to guard private enterprises and property rights as well as maintaining its hold on power. The carrot-and-stick strategy of politely meeting with the activists but arresting one of them afterward quickly suppressed the original protest. Some female collective workers, however, took over the protest and redirected it.

When the Shaowu Sawmill workers first demonstrated on January 26, they drew no clear distinction between the state workers and collective workers: they were families, neighbors, and friends who had all been leading difficult lives after the layoffs. When the activists first met with government representatives, they had not prepared for bargaining. Instead of outlining demands agreed on by the group, the ten activists who spontaneously joined in the meeting talked individually about an extensive range of issues. These issues included the land sale, the low severance pay, the inefficiency of governmental bureaucrats in processing their retirement benefits, ongoing housing problems, and the difficulties disabled workers faced after being laid off. One of the first-generation state workers mentioned that a plot of land along the river where the wooden crate workshop had stood, redeveloped by a real estate company called Jianxin in the early 2000s, had been originally reclaimed and built by the collective workers in the early 1980s. "Collective workers," he urged, "the land along the river is your land. You all should fight to have it back!" This statement was taken seriously by collective workers, who realized that their identity and legal standing were different from the laid-off state workers.

The January 26 demonstration took place four days before the 2014 Lunar New Year. During the New Year's celebrations and gatherings, the women former collective workers ran into each other and chatted about the demonstration and the meeting. News spread quickly and easily, since everyone still lived in the work-unit apartment complex. Accustomed to living and working together, related by blood or friendship, the women gradually agreed that this might be an excellent opportunity for them to reclaim their assets and ask for more compensation.

The women collective workers had long shared the experiences of lower-paid positions, condescension from their state worker counterparts, and difficulties in reemployment, but partly because many of them were married to state workers and shared the household income, they had not realized that their separate employment status might in fact prove advantageous for claiming compensation. They began to align themselves more firmly with the legal classification of "collective workers" in order to strengthen their claims to property and land rights under the post-Mao regulations.[2]

As the women chatted, those who were born in the early 1960s, had a middle-school education, and had already reached the legal retirement age (and thus started receiving pensions) emerged as the activists among the group. They consulted friends and acquaintances who worked in real estate and law. Online research revealed two major legal provisions supporting their position. First, the People's Republic of China Urban Collective-Owned Enterprise Regulations asserted the employees' collective ownership of means of production and accumulated assets: land, buildings, machines and equipment, tools, and raw materials. Second, it is widely known that in the People's Republic of China, the state owns urban land, while peasant collectives own rural land. But it is less well-known that urban collective-owned land exists, and for a collective enterprise, the employees are the collective landowners.

Knowing their legal grounds, the activists started taking action: they made a list of assets owned by the collective enterprise, and the five leading activists, all women, wrote a petition expressing their grievances and demanding redress, and then gathered individual signatures and fingerprints. This process also entailed educating one another about legal matters and recalling the injustices they had experienced during and after the sawmill privatization. In doing so, the women effectively constructed a collective consciousness and bolstered their confidence and determination.

After the two hundred activists jostled past the police officers and flooded into the city hall on February 26, a month after the first big demonstration at the mill, they were unable to find the mayor's office. Apparently its location had been deliberately omitted from the building directory sign. After some chaotic wandering around, forty women protesters gathered in a random conference room, loudly demanding for about an hour to meet the mayor. Finally, the forestry department director, acting as the city government representative, came and talked with them. He appeared unconcerned and started confidently reciting the Shaowu Sawmill's history to show his understanding of the current situation, as well as his capacity for managing it. He asserted that because the collective enterprise was built by a state enterprise as a way to create jobs for employees' children, its assets belonged to the state, and the workers did not have any claims on them.

The activists quickly pointed out the holes in the director's argument. The collective enterprise workers and state workers labored in the same factory and contributed to the sawmill and the state in the same way. But when the mill became privatized, the collective workers were laid off earlier and with much less compensation. Because the Shaowu Sawmill had paid less into the collective workers' social security, the collective workers received monthly pension payments of only around ¥800, one-third of what the average state worker received. The collective workers made their point clear: "If you think we are no different from the state workers, pay us back the social security and keep our pension as high as our state worker equivalents. If not, acknowledge that our positions are different from those of the state workers and admit that we were collective workers and our unit was a collective enterprise, the assets of which were legally categorized and regulated differently." Then they read aloud the relevant statute of the People's Republic of China Urban Collective-Owned Enterprise Regulations to support their claim to ownership of the collective enterprise land and buildings. They also read their collective petition aloud: "Relying on the income of our temporary jobs [after being laid off], which is extremely low, we have managed to sustain ourselves until now. We suffered without complaint, believing in the party and the government. But today, all of us workers are shocked and devastated, and our anger is finally breaking out. We found that our assets were sold during privatization in 2000, in secret and at a low price."

The collective workers had known for a long time that the Shaowu Sawmill assets had been sold; what they had not known was that they had claims to these assets. Therefore, when they said they were "shocked and devastated," they were expressing emotions that were not new but had built up over sixteen years. The people who seemed really shocked at the meeting were the Forestry Department director and a vice mayor, who had arrived at the meeting half an hour after the director. They had not heard of these legal regulations before, and certainly they did not expect the retired women to be so smart and knowledgeable. Seeing their awkwardness, the forty women activists became more confident and raised their voices, chanting, "We want our assets back!" Tongue-tied and ashamed, the two male officials had to agree to the activists' demand to create a task force to examine this case. The women pushed the two officials to write down their agreement: the investigation would start the next day and include worker representatives.

Throughout the months following this demonstration, the five lead activists went to the Forestry Department office or the city hall daily for updates from the task force and to push for further actions. They went through the mill documents and account books with the accountants and police officers sent by the city government and the Forestry Department. In March, the collective workers met and elected thirty-six representatives, including the five original leaders. This group of five leaders met frequently to give updates and plan the next steps, and then all thirty-six representatives reported back to their neighbors and networks. Because they lived in different apartment buildings and worked at different workshops, they could quickly disseminate the news to all the former sawmill workers. They used digital platforms like QQ and WeChat for communication as well. They usually shared news and facts quickly and accurately. However, occasionally some people were misinformed, and, especially when progress was slow, some people worried that the lead activists were neglecting their duties.

In late March the city government assigned a lawyer named Yang to "offer the laid-off workers professional legal consultation." As a government agent, Yang focused on persuading the activists to give up their struggle. After one of the meetings with the lawyer and the Forestry Department vice director, the lead activists became extremely frustrated. Lina, who was among them, lashed out: "It's already been over a month. They [the officials] are still trying to brush us off. The lawyer is totally on their side too, and he was sent to patronize us. He is a lawyer, but when we talked about legal regulations with him, he told us to think about the particularity of the history. However, when we discussed the history of the mill, he switched to addressing the legal institution's difficulties in resolving our issues."

When the activists cited specific law, the lawyer told them that these provisions were enacted either too early in the Maoist era to apply to reform-era events or too recently to apply to past events. He asked the activists to consider the unique transition of China, stressing that the concepts of ownership and property law were both new to the People's Republic of China and thus could not apply to collective enterprises. However, when the activists invoked the history of the mill, pointing out that collective and state workers once worked side by side, to support their request for pensions commensurate with those of state workers, the lawyer replied that the status assigned them by the Maoist institution was unchangeable, even if it had been a mistake.

The state and its laws created a double jeopardy for the collective workers.[3] On the one hand, their arguments that their past labor was equivalent to that of state workers, and therefore deserving of equal compensation, were undermined by the dominant post-Mao understanding of PRC history which held that the country was absolutely different before and after the late-1970s reform. The official party discourse, including Jiang Zemin's exhortation to "advance with the times" (*yu shi ju jin*), together with popular culture and scholarly works, all reinforced the idea that people needed to move on and leave the past behind. Maoism, with its emphasis on class struggle and wrongly radical socialism, would not benefit the modern nation's development.[4] This state-engineered historiography effectively erased all the contributions made by the workers and peasants during the period of Maoist capital accumulation and sent the message that all the labor that contributed to Mao-era economic development was disposable.

The activists' counterargument was that if they were not considered equal with state workers, they must be seen as collective workers; therefore they had an ownership stake in the mill and were entitled to a share of the revenue from its sale. In post-Mao China, however, although property rights were increasingly protected under the law, the state workers and collective workers who had been called the owners of the entire country were stripped of rights and left behind in the disposable past. The lawyer and the City of Shaowu used both systems to create a double bind for the women collective workers.

As Lina's comments show, the activists clearly understood and articulated the intersectional institutional oppressions that they encountered. They pushed the city government to choose either the socialist discourse of fairness or the postsocialist legal framework of ownership. In choosing the former, the government would have to recognize their labor contribution to the previous state enterprise and the national economy and pay them compensation and pensions equal to those of state workers. In choosing the latter, the government would have to validate their collective ownership of the land and other assets of the collective enterprise and pay them part of the land-sale revenue.

Lina's comments show how the activists articulated the constructed dichotomy imposed on them. They rejected the government's intention to define history as a linear timeline in which the socialist discourse of labor and justice was relegated to the past and was thus inapplicable to workers in the reform era, while the postsocialist law was not considered to cover situations before the reform. Through their activism, the women collective workers deepened their understanding of the state practice of creating social stratification in order to control the labor force and enhance economic development. Moreover, they became more skilled in knowing what discourses and tactics they could use to negotiate with the government.

Different Tactics

In drafting the petition letter for the February 26 demonstration, the activists considered the discussions during the January 24 demonstration, when the sawmill workers had talked about their various life experiences and expressed resentment about the enterprise privatization, "sending the national assets to some private owners" and "sacrificing the old workers who had contributed to the country." To increase their chance of success, the activists decided to focus on four demands they felt best represented the interests of the majority of laid-off collective workers and were most likely to be fulfilled by the city government:

1. A portion of the sales revenue from the land and assets
   of the collective enterprise
2. Higher pensions
3. Increased severance pay
4. Resolution of housing problems

On the day of the demonstration, the activists tried to represent all women collective workers by voicing their resentment about their treatment during the layoffs and their suffering afterward—although they agreed that "it was necessary to restructure the state enterprises" to achieve national economic growth. They then pointed out the legal grounds for their demands.

A month later, the activists held a meeting to update the laid-off collective workers and mobilize additional support. This time the sole focus was on the law. After explaining their legal claims, Lina waved a photocopy of the legal provision protecting collective workers' assets in her right hand and called out, "Did you all hear this? This is our right! No one can violate it. How can the government intervene and sell our collective-owned land and assets? We want to fight back for our assets!" Two hundred women enthusiastically responded.

From January to March, the activists' discourse narrowed. The narrative criticizing privatization and the recounting of individual experiences gave way to the collective claim of property rights. In joint actions, activists often ended up focusing on only a few demands to make their political goals more achievable. But what did that mean in the context of Chinese social and legal transformation?

In China, instead of openly defying the authoritarian state, protesters often creatively use national laws, central government policies, provincial regulations, leadership speeches, and other Party-promoted values to pressure local governments. They carefully avoid actions that could be interpreted as unlawful and thus weaken their standing.[5] Often protesting groups assert their social and economic rights rather than civil and political rights. For instance, when a group of homeowners protested against the construction of a new building in their neighborhood park in Guangzhou, they publicly claimed to be "protecting their environmental rights." They also claimed to be working in partnership with the central state in defending the law and correcting the legal transgressions of the local government. The resident activists avoided being seen as arguing for political freedom.[6] The Shaowu activists said, "We should make [the government] notice us but should not let them lose face." These tactics of "depoliticized politics" helped the activists keep their legitimacy under the current framework of laws and rules.

A collective workers' rally at which Lina (in the foreground) informed other workers of their rights, 2014.

Although it is a safer mode of protest than outright defiance, using the law as a basis for oppositional actions in China runs the risk of activists' being co-opted into the state "legal construction" (*fazhi jianshe*) project, by which all kinds of societal grievances are seen as claims for narrowly defined legal rights based on existing laws. The Taishi Village recall campaign, documented in Ai Xiaoming's internationally distributed film *Taishi*, is a good example. In 2005, the residents of Taishi Village in Guangdong attempted to recall the incumbent village leader, who was suspected of embezzlement. The campaigners tried to "vernacularize" the laws relating to village governance by linking them to the collectivist past of the village and a vision of building a moral community.[7] However, the lawyers and outside activists who spoke for them constructed the dispute as concerning only a legal and democratic voting process, and this was the interpretation transmitted through international media and activist networks. This approach not only limited the solution to the realm of law and constitutionalism (which gave the state a means of rejecting the recall) but also silenced the villagers, especially the older women, who had been active in the campaign for broader moral reasons and had endured several days of hunger strikes and police violence.

Similarly, the workers laid off from the Shaowu Sawmill saw their multi-directional grievances recast as a single legal dispute over property rights. But their actions were not based solely on legal claims. In private, several activists told me that they believed in neither the legal system nor the idea that the current Chinese laws promote justice. In an authoritarian society, citizens' rights are limited, and their power is circumscribed. The government defines legality. Even a city government official alluded to this fact when debating with the activists: "You always talk about the laws. Why do you believe in the laws that much? Why can you not believe in the government?" To defy the local government, they had to be strategic in the use of "the master's tools."[8]

Lina summarized for me what the activists had learned from negotiating with the government: "We cannot see the government as a government. We need to see it as a company or a businessman. Now we want to take money out of their pockets, and any businessman would hate this. So we must be strategic." They understood that the Chinese state does not prioritize the interests of citizens or public goods. The local government, as an economic entity, pursues its own interests. Both the citizens and the government are constrained and protected by the law, but the government has much more power in interpreting and changing the law. The use of a legal narrative made the collective voice of these women worker-activists less radical and publicly critical, but negotiating with the government on legal grounds strengthened and sharpened the individual activists' critical analysis of the role of the government and legal institutions in Chinese state capitalism.

At the same time, the activists honored all the truths of the laid-off workers' position. Although they strategically focused on collective property rights, they also argued for equal pensions and talked about the significance of their labor contributions to the former state enterprise. They constantly shifted between different lenses through which to view their experiences.

They were able to switch between different ideologies and tactics because they had long been politically conscious of the diverse forms of oppression they had experienced in both the Mao and post-Mao times. They were ready to change tactics as the dynamics of the situation dictated.[9] The ideologies they had inherited from collectivization, privatization, socialism, and capitalism gave them a tool for every job. They switched between speaking bitterness about previous work, the legal framework of property rights, and the moral argument about the equality of individuals. None of these tactics singlehandedly solved their problems, but all were useful.

During the campaign, they gained support from unexpected sources. One vital piece of evidence they obtained was an agreement showing that the city government had allocated a piece of land to a developer for free.

The fifteenth of each month is Meet the Mayor Day in Shaowu. The mayor and directors of all major government departments are available in a conference room at the Letters and Complaints Bureau to meet with residents who have petitions or complaints. This practice is a legacy of the socialist era. There is usually a long line, so when the five lead sawmill activists decided to attend the session on April 15, 2014, they went at 6:30 a.m. They would have only fifteen minutes to talk with the city officials, so as they waited they discussed strategies for presenting their grievances and how best to use their supporting evidence.

As they waited, a man passed by and entered the meeting room. They quickly recognized him as Hong, the Shaowu Sawmill director at the time when the state and collective mill enterprises were sold between 1998 and 2000. The activists immediately shifted their strategy.

In February the government had agreed to an investigation of the sale of the land along the river that had been filled in by the collective workers. Leading activists had joined the police officers and government officials in examining the collective enterprise's archives. I was there, and since the government officials had brought a camcorder, the activists asked me to record the investigation as well, so they would have their own video documentation of the process. At first, the only documents found pertained to the establishment of the collective enterprise, recruitment, and the layoffs— nothing too surprising. Around noon, we stopped for a lunch break, and the officials left us alone. One of the activists excitedly took out a paper she had secreted in her pocket: "Look what I found! These bastards gave our land to the [Jianxin] real estate developer for free! The government and the big factory [a term for the sawmill state-sector leadership] did this together."

The person who had signed the agreement on behalf of the city government and the sawmill was Hong. No one assumed he was the only or the most important figure involved in transferring the land to the developer.

Still, when he showed up on Meet the Mayor Day, the activists realized they could target some individuals from the leadership who had participated in the deal. This strategy might be more effective than presenting the evidence and legal provisions of collective asset ownership. Besides, the activists frankly admitted to me that they simply enjoyed the chance to embarrass the government officials.

When their turn came to meet with the city leaders, the activists reviewed the history of the collective enterprise of the Shaowu Sawmill and how they had been treated differently from the state workers before, during, and after privatization. They supported their claim to the assets using legal provisions. When they began to run out of time, Lina pulled out a photocopy of the land-allocation agreement and announced: "I want to show you all a strange agreement. The land along the river, where the Jianxin residential apartments are located now, was the land of the collective enterprise, was part of our land. However, this agreement shows that in 2000, the land was given away to the Jianxin Real Estate Company by the city government and the state enterprise of Shaowu Sawmill, without any clear agreement from the collective enterprise. Let's look at the signature on the agreement: the person representing the government and the seller's side was the Shaowu Sawmill director at that time, Hong."

People in the room burst out laughing.

Lina pretended to be confused and asked: "Why are you all laughing? Did I say anything wrong?" Someone pointed at Hong and said, "That is him, the person you just mentioned."

"Oh, I'm sorry. I didn't recognize you or know you were here," Lina continued, playing the innocent. "I'm not against you. I'm aiming at discussing the issue per se." She got specific, pointing out the conflict: "We had lower severance pay and pensions because we were considered 'purely collective workers.' But if we are 'purely collective workers,' our land is collectively owned by us workers. In that case, we request Jianxin Real Estate to return our land to us; otherwise, the land allocation was undoubtedly illegal, and we demand an investigation."

Even before she finished her sentence, one of the deputy mayors jumped up and said, "It was wrong that you were all registered as collective workers. You are not 'purely collective workers,' and you should all be considered state workers as well. The Social Security Department, you guys should come and solve this problem." After that, the officials smiled in a kindly fashion and dismissed the activists, promising their issue would be solved soon.

The leading activists were excited. They believed the deputy mayor had participated in the land transaction: why else would he be so eager to interrupt Lina and rush to resolve the problem? According to the Chinese land law, the government can allocate lands for military use, infrastructure construction, and other public welfare projects, but not to business units or for-profit organizations. Although the activists were disappointed with the officials' corruption and illegality, exposing their wrongdoing wasn't their goal. All they wanted was government compensation, either an increase in their pensions or payment from the land sale. A few weeks after this meeting, in May, the city government agreed to compensate the women workers a lump sum of ¥17,000,000 for the land and buildings the workers were claiming.

Corruption has been a major social and political issue in China since the late 1970s, and the practice of resource allocation by both the state and the market was considered the primary cause. To avoid political instability and a legitimacy crisis for the regime, to increase the transparency and efficiency of the market and enhance economic development, and to attract more international investment, the Chinese central government has engineered several waves of anticorruption campaigns.[10] The laid-off state workers, who had been disadvantaged by the state's capitalist economic policies, were able to use the party campaigns—recently refashioned by capitalist economic incentives—to amplify their own political voices.

Timing

To return to the questions that opened this chapter: Why did the women workers wait sixteen years to begin their collective resistance? How could they unite in this cause when the workforce had been disbanded for such a long time? And what made 2014 a turning point?

For over a decade, I have listened to the laid-off workers complain about their living situations and working conditions. Disappointment with their lives stretches back to enterprise privatization, if not before. But when they were laid off, they faced oppression from the policies of both the central and the local governments. The power differential was dramatic. When many state enterprises were privatized around 2000 in northern Fujian, almost all factory worker groups protested to some extent. The local governments either detained the leading activists and even publicly beat them as a warning to others, or they ignored the workers. The Shaowu Sawmill collective women workers had conducted a sit-in demonstration in front of the city hall for three days in 1998. The city government warned them that if any of them broke the law by blocking the road, they would be arrested; otherwise, they could sit as long as they wanted. Other than that, the government kept silent. At that time, many of the laid-off workers had school-age children. Education and childcare had been privatized and cost more. In the post-Mao era, education was seen as essential to success in the job market, so the laid-off workers gave up protesting and focused their energies on looking for new jobs to support their children's schooling. Many of them said: "Our generation has been destroyed. We will not have much success anyway. So if our suffering can give our children a good future, we feel it's worth it." Moreover, they saw no way to outlast the city government with their protests.

But sixteen years later, the tables had turned. Almost all laid-off women workers had reached the retirement age of fifty. Their children were grown and no longer needed their financial support. The women had more time and energy to negotiate with the city government. Only half joking, the activists told the government officials: "We have nothing but time!" When they needed people to demonstrate in front of the city hall, they could quickly call out two hundred. The five leading protesters went to the Forestry Department every day, sometimes staying in the director's office peacefully complaining for long periods. The workers in effect turned the "unproductive" time of old age and retirement into a socially productive force. They could outlast the government.

Many collective actions in China have adopted this strategy. The Societies of Senior Citizens (ssc) was the major group opposing a 2005 plan to build chemical plants in Zhejiang Village. Because of the age of its members, the ssc enjoyed the advantages of substantial autonomy, financial resources, and strong, experienced leadership. At that time about 20 percent of the villagers were ssc members, and both the law and Chinese custom grant privileges and respect to those aged seventy or more.[11] In the hunger strike that was part of the 2015 Taishi Village recall campaign, elderly women were the major participants. Although their voices were silenced in the international discussion of this protest, Ai Xiaoming's film illustrated the gendered poverty in the village and the older women's active participation in the campaign.[12]

Age is one of the reasons why the male workers did not participate in the protest, even though 5 to 10 percent of the collective workers were men. The legal retirement age for men is sixty, so many of the men were still working. In addition, male workers told me that men were more likely to be targeted by police violence because they were seen as a more significant threat than women. Some women activists gave me a more amusing explanation: "Because men are all cowards, and we women are fearless." This answer was partly a criticism of some male workers who didn't participate in the protest yet were dismissive of the women's efforts.

One day during the negotiations with the government, a former male colleague invited the leading activists to dinner and gave them advice: "Even if you continue making a fuss, you are just wasting your time." He agreed that privatization had been handled badly, since it sent so many workers back home. "But how can the state let you, a group of women, win by making all these noises? Just use your brain to think it over. How is it possible? If you achieve your goal, I will swallow this beer bottle." He waved his bottle. Right after the women workers learned that the local government had agreed to pay the compensation they had demanded, a couple of activists joked: "We should bring him a beer bottle to swallow now!"

The activists used a range of feminized tactics. After the layoffs, the five leading activists had all worked in positions that required relationship building and frequent customer interactions. This work experience improved their skills in dealing with people from different backgrounds, including government officials. During their negotiations, they always reminded one another that some of them needed to be confrontational and stubborn, while others needed to adopt a softer approach. After every fight with the officials, at least one of them needed to step forward and offer some face-saving kind words in order to continue the negotiation. "We all dislike the government, but we want the government to do things for us. It's just like being friends with your enemy." They skillfully employed a "good cop, bad cop" strategy.

Their sixteen years of post-layoff life, particularly the discrimination they faced in the new labor market and their difficulty in getting government assistance, had convinced them that the state no longer existed to serve the people. China now is building its economy through capitalist accumulation and exploitation of surplus value. Manual laborers are not the beneficiaries of this project. Even after the city government's agreement to give them ¥17,000,000, the activists stayed cool-headed. Lina considered the victory "not a true victory, but just a small thing, which doesn't cause much change, because we are still living at the very bottom of the society, and because our country's institutions are problematic." The activists were aware that their victory relied on legal institutions and did not challenge the institutions themselves. Using legal tools in their activism, the activists developed "a better sense of [their] rights but with reduced belief in the law as a capable protector of those rights."[13] Their changed understanding of the state, government, legal institutions, and economic development enabled these activists to critically analyze their position in the economy and pursue collective action. In the words of another lead activist, Chen Meimei: "After this protest, our minds became so clear. If we had had this kind of consciousness sixteen years ago, they could not have privatized our factory so easily."

However, there was a problem with their strategy. When the Shaowu government promised to compensate the protesters ¥17,000,000, the group automatically agreed to drop all other claims, such as pension adjustments. The city government had promised the activists to pay the compensation once they had sold the rest of the sawmill land to a real estate developer. When the activists began to protest in early 2014, the sawmill land was estimated to be worth over ¥100,000,000, because housing prices were high. The collective enterprise constituted one-fifth of that land, worth about ¥20,000,000. In the summer of 2014, when both parties were trying to settle the compensation agreement, the real-estate bubble burst. The land, now worth less than ¥50,000,000, couldn't be sold because the city had long promised the privately owned mills that each of them would receive over ¥10,000,000 from the sale.

In summer 2014, the laid-off workers negotiated with the government to take over three buildings that had been owned by the collective enterprise before 1998. They decided to rent out the buildings until the government sold the land and compensated them. By the end of 2016, then rental earnings amounted to ¥300,000, which was shared among five hundred collective workers.

Meanwhile, many retired workers planted vegetable gardens on the land where the demolished mill buildings and equipment had stood, mostly to feed their own families and sometimes to sell produce in the farmers' market. Hundreds of small agricultural plots lay among the remaining workshop buildings and walls. The retired workers were happy about the daily harvest. It's perhaps a good example of the working class disrupting the regular operation of state capitalism: the left-out workers reused the industrial land where they had once worked. On the other hand, the production of plywood over the decades had involved extensive use of toxic chemicals. No one acknowledged the hidden dangers of using polluted land for agriculture. Perhaps the specter of lingering toxins in the workers' rice bowls is a symbol of how Mao-era unequal labor relations still affect the workers today.

In summer 2017, the city finally sold the land and declared it was ready to pay the laid-off workers, contingent on the workers' presenting a collective agreement stating how the compensation would be divided. Officials further emphasized: "If even one worker comes to the government to make a fuss about the way of distributing money, the government won't give out the money." Beginning around 2004, the Chinese government, under Hu Jintao and Xi Jinping, has invested hundreds of billions of yuan in building administrative structures, surveillance systems, and professional teams to maintain social stability. That entails suppressing domestic dissent, and the local government—the first line of defense—wanted to forestall any potential future objection. In this case, the local government delegated this task to the collective workers themselves, particularly the lead activists.

The requirement of a collective agreement was also a divide-and-conquer strategy intended to cause conflicts among the workers—which it did. The older generation argued that the money should be divided according to how long each person had worked in the sawmill—a logic typical of the Mao era, when seniority was the primary determinant of workers' salaries. Of course the younger generation disagreed. They reminded the older generation of an odd difference between them: because the sawmill had paid social security for the workers who had retired before the 1998 privatization, most of the first-generation collective workers, who had been "family dependents," had much higher pensions than the rest. Nobody could explain why the administration had made this distinction. But it made many younger people believe they should now be compensated more than the elders.

This intergenerational conflict was not the only disagreement. The sawmill administration had made its last attempt at "gentle" restructuring in 1997, before the collective enterprise was completely privatized. It proposed changing the enterprise collective into a corporate enterprise by making all employees into stockholders, and it required each worker to pay a minimum of ¥3,000 to buy stock (see chapter 4). Most collective workers paid the money, despite the financial hardship it imposed, because they wanted to keep their jobs. Those who refused to purchase the stock were asked to resign. Of course, those who did pay the money lost their jobs a year later anyway. But the question remained whether those who had quit their jobs before the privatization should share the land-sale money. After all, their labor relations with the enterprise had ceased in 1997. And a final question was whether families of those workers who had passed away after 1998 should be counted in.

What is justice? The workers were forced to wrestle long and hard with this question. Should the compensation be paid according to need, seniority, length of service, the degree of hardship experienced as a result of the policy, or existing labor relations? How could these women choose among the many ideologies that steered their lives?

Toward the end of 2019, these questions were resolved (maybe only temporarily) with an agreement that everybody, regardless of generation or whether they had paid the investment money, would divide the compensation equally. The city government and the Department of Forestry, however, refused to honor their earlier agreement. With the government leadership completely changed, they now questioned the legitimacy of the workers' representatives selected through the 2014 voting process.

Lina, hospitalized for her uremia, called me in December 2020 asking me to send the videos I had made during the voting. The videos showed not only the entire process but also the Forestry Department officials' monitoring of it, and the activists wanted to use them as evidence. Lina told me this time they might need to pursue a lawsuit against the city government. None of the activists had much faith in this lawsuit, but they had enough rage to do it.

With the help of a hired lawyer, the activists attempted to file a lawsuit against the Forestry Department at the Shaowu City Court. However, the court denied this lawsuit. Back to their old tactic, the activists went to the Forestry Department and city hall once every few days between 2021 and 2023. (Lina didn't participate in these visits anymore because of her declining health but she was kept in the loop when significant changes happened.)

Finally, in the autumn of 2023, the City of Shaowu agreed to compensate all collective workers who had employment status with the Shaowu Sawmill at the time it was sold. That is to say, the workers who retired before that and those workers who refused to pay the investment money and were forced to quit in 1997 could not get the money. The city government transferred ¥17,900,000 from the sawmill land's sale revenue to the Forestry Department in December 2023 to fund this compensation.

Between December 20 and December 31, the activists set up a table in a corner of a small convenience store (currently managed by a former collective worker) at the ground level of one of the skyscraper apartment buildings that had been built on the former sawmill land. Over five hundred collective workers handed in their identification card photocopies, bank account information, and documents that could demonstrate their employment status with the sawmill in 1998. The Forestry Department promised to transfer money directly into each worker's bank account in the first half of 2024. My book couldn't capture the final status of these transfers, but it contains my optimism that the workers can finally receive compensation after such a decades-long fight.

EPILOGUE

The summer of 2018 was the first time I took my child back to Shaowu. We stayed at the Dragon Lake Forest Farm for ten days to enable me to conduct follow-up interviews, as well as to escape from the heat in the city. My one-and-a-half-year-old was fascinated by the plants, birds, and especially bugs that we encountered at the farm. We strictly followed the farm employees' guidance on which parts of the river were safe to take a dip in, because in many places the riverbed had been damaged by construction projects, and the river currents had become extremely dangerous for swimmers. Although my family brought some food from urban Shaowu, much of it went bad quickly because there was no refrigerator available, so we began purchasing food from farm employees who grew vegetables and raised poultry.

We had gone into the mountains with a group of former forest farm workers, but they left after a short weekend stay because the farm, though full of beautiful memories, was too "boring" and "crude." After their departure, a group of college students arrived for a one-week environmental education camp organized by educators from the Wilderness Society, a nonprofit organization based in Taiwan. To increase revenue, the farm had started a semipublic ecotourism business, mainly marketed toward nostalgic former employees and the newly developed environmental education industry. This camp was a training opportunity for college students who wanted to start their own local environmental education activities. Its main purpose was to improve their skills in teaching about insects and spiders. The Wuyi mountain range is known for its abundance of insects, and there are over one hundred types of spiders in the region. The camp participants had no knowledge or interest in the history of the local forestry reforms and labor politics, although they did ask questions about forest conservation and ecotourism. To them, this was an ahistorical space, one that allowed them to take advantage of nature in an area with high bio-diversity. Ironically, at a time when Chinese state forestry is transitioning from production to conservation, human communities are being physically and culturally separated from the forests, and their stories are also being removed from the narrative of the land.

In saying this, I am not singling out environmental educators for criticism. Even though I come from the Wuyi Mountains and grew up in the forestry community, I knew little of the history of forestry labor. I heard adults in the Shaowu Sawmill talk about *song mu* (Chinese red pine), *shan mu* (China fir), *zhu zi* (bamboo), and *za mu* (miscellaneous plants), and I saw logs, plywood, and particleboard. But I knew nothing about the migration of the workers, the gendered division of labor, or how my community's labor has fundamentally changed the natural, social, and economic landscapes of my hometown. I was humbled to listen to these women talk about their lives. Their stories and their own interpretations of their stories have renewed my identity as a part of a working-class community and changed my comprehension of Chinese economy and history.

First and foremost, I was impressed by all the difficulties experienced by the earlier generations of forestry workers, which included my parents and grandparents. As they frequently remarked: "Everything we believed when we were fifteen, we don't believe now that we are fifty." I sympathized with their feelings of disorientation through all the changes, and I observed how hard they worked to find new meaning for their lives and create new value systems. I struggled with the fear that I couldn't honor their stories in the right way. Behind these individuals' experiences and feelings lay their need to address and resist structural oppression. Many of these women's narratives demonstrate that the narrators understood their oppression and the way it was constructed. And even though the dominant discourse of development has suppressed this kind of storytelling, the narrators are unwilling to stop talking about the actual value of their labor. They are inspiring.

Meanwhile, it was thrilling to watch their individual narratives and feelings coalesce into collective action. The women were able to keep speaking to audiences unwilling to listen to them anymore, recalling their histories and reminding the state officials of the value they had created for the country. Such stories, told by oppressed groups, challenge the dominant narrative of economic development. In particular, the forestry workers' stories reveal the mechanisms by which the state manufactured and utilized dichotomies—humans versus nature, urban versus rural, men versus women—to expropriate and exploit land, labor, and forests in the cause of capital accumulation. These manufactured dichotomies manifested themselves continuously across the Mao and post-Mao eras, although the divisions changed slightly over time.

The Continuity of Oppression

Some versions of history told by the Chinese government and international mainstream media have constructed a complete rupture between the Mao and post-Mao eras in China. In forestry, for example, the state has regulated land, forest resources, labor, and production in a rather different manner following privatization. However, behind all the apparent differences, many mechanisms for capital accumulation are common to the two periods.

In Maoist China, these included policies guided by Mao's assertion that "humanity is destined to conquer nature." With those policies, the forests became a free resource that could and should be exploited by socialist industrialization. Second, capital accumulation by the state relied on forest tenure collectivization and privileging urban industry over rural villages. When the state deprived rural people of the means to meet their basic needs, uprooting peasants from their land became much easier. Third, under the planned economy, the state set the prices of raw materials and labor along the supply chain to maximize the capital the state could accumulate.

In the post-Mao era, capital accumulation was enabled by the privatization of forest property rights and wood-processing enterprises, which co-opted environmentalist concerns about deforestation. In addition, privatization efforts benefited from the Maoist legacies that had culturally and socially divorced state workers, peasants, and new rural migrants from the forests and the rural villages. Hence the forests became simply property that villagers could cash in on to escape the inadequate infrastructure, unfulfilled basic needs, and internalized discrimination against rural people that had come to characterize village life. Subsequently the forests were subjected to strong state control.

Both eras were also marked by gendered labor exploitation. When wives were defined as dependents and given primary responsibility for caring labor, their removal from their home villages and cultural environment was framed as a state benefit for the men. As a result, women's work was devalued. Wives' positions and conditions were passed down to daughters, and the gendered labor divisions in the state enterprises continued after privatization.

Even though the dynamics of the situation have changed over time, understanding these divides and how they have guided policies and discourses is a prerequisite to comprehending social hierarchy and inequalities in China. The forestry industry presents a rare opportunity to examine all of these dichotomies at once and study the interconnections. Furthermore, the same dichotomies exist in many economies and societies around the world. Comparative studies across economies could help to illustrate the mechanisms of structural oppression and capital accumulation on a global scale.

Imperfect Resistance

The women forestry workers strategically used discourses and tactics from various historical and political contexts, including the new era of state capitalism. Their wisdom, drawn from their personal stories and understanding of their own values, resulted in successful negotiations against the local government. Their adaptability and strength send a positive signal to workers' movements around the globe.

Yet to avoid forming a romanticized narrative of the triumph of working-class and feminist resistance, it is important to acknowledge and examine the divisions and conflicts among the laid-off state workers. Both men and women workers were harmed by the privatization of the sawmill and oppressed by the capitalist economy. The women workers could find new work only in low-paid positions. The men faced either continued employment in the privately owned factories where they were not respected, or unemployment or precarious employment that undermined their status as family breadwinners. The entire working class hurt. Such pain is often diagnosed as a symptom of interpersonal conflict between men, the "failed breadwinners," and women, the "unskilled labor," rather than the result of systemic labor exploitation.

Intergenerational miscommunications and estrangements were evident within the forestry community. When the state abdicated responsibility for eldercare, my grandmother's decades of speaking bitterness—a strategy she had used to support her family—started to sound to her children like constant complaining. When her children also suffered the consequences of privatization, the mutual misunderstanding and resentment grew. These intergenerational frictions are not merely personal dramas but micro-manifestations of macroeconomic reforms and ideological changes. The state's intentional disposal of successive generations of laborers created family conflict.

Conflicts also existed among the three groups of people who earned a living from the forests and the wood processing industry: the state forestry workers, the local Fujianese peasants, and the migrant workers from China's southwest. Forestry reforms, particularly in forest tenure, regularly pitted forestry workers and peasants against each other. The first-generation state forestry workers were also migrants, coming from rural regions in the 1950s and 1960s. Despite all the difficulties they and their communities went through, they retained some of the privileges of their employment during the collectivization era. Even if they are now unemployed, they have stable housing, urban household registration, local and long-term social networks, and a small but reliable pension income. The new wave of migrant workers that came to Fujian in the 1990s has been less fortunate, facing hostility from both the peasants and the state logging camp workers. For instance, the local peasants did not want the "dangerous strangers" to live near their villages. The state farm patrols have detained the new migrant workers for illegal logging, even when the patrols knew that private tree farmers, either local villagers (like Huang, discussed in chapter 3) or outside business owners were really behind the activity.

Workers around the world have been pitted against each other through global economic competition. Women in different situations may approach feminist agendas in very different, even oppositional ways. Chinese state forestry workers were estranged from each other by gender, generation, and place of origin — this last point of difference being of course reinforced by the state-constructed categories of "rural" and "urban" workers.

The dominant American narrative positions Chinese workers as a group who stole jobs from US Rust Belt workers in the 1990s. Western leftists increasingly look to Chinese workers as offering hope for a revived international workers' movement. Both these discourses take account only of workers in the export-oriented factories.[1] They overlook retired and laid-off state workers, together with Maoism, seeing them as irrelevant to economic growth and workers' activism. The focus on international economic competition has obscured the globalized exploitation of all working-class people and the intentional construction of vulnerable labor subjects.

Despite structural oppressions, workers are neither homogeneous nor submissive. The life stories of the collective workers show that Maoism itself was gendered, and that it had uneven influences on different women's everyday lives and consciousness. Yet these women repurposed the Maoist state-governance techniques to meet their own needs. I feel honored to have witnessed and stood with them while their individual storytelling coalesced into collective resistance.

Envisioning a Movement Centering Care

Driven by the goal of capital accumulation during both the Maoist and the post-Maoist years, the Chinese economy has pitted humans against nature, urban residents against rural, male against female, young against old, and material production against human compassion and caring. Through these constructed and intertwined dualities, Maoist and post-Maoist development has capitalized on marginalization. Laborers, divided from each other ideologically and materially, have been prevented from presenting a united front.

How might we envision a different kind of economy and a different activist agenda? First, the status and benefits of paid employment would not be the only or even the primary goal of activism. Labor activism that is mainly concerned with formal employment status typically excludes or marginalizes the needs of many providers of care labor (primarily women).

Moreover, when labor activism focuses on job opportunities and material benefits, a sense of scarcity often pits different groups of workers against one another.

Institutions driven by capital accumulation intentionally draw the line between profitable, productive tasks and unprofitable caring duties. Devaluing the latter category of work is a way to maximize surplus value. In Shaowu, the family dependent workers' tasks of planting and caring for trees were less valued than the state workers' logging and factory tasks. An alternative model of labor politics would discard the profit-centered logic of creating competition and disposability among laborers.

How would the lives of Chinese forestry workers look within such a model of labor politics? If domestic and outside labor were equally valued, men would no longer be cast as breadwinners, and losing productive-sector employment would no longer set off recriminations based on gender roles. If current and past labor were equally valued, the economy could properly reward the work of caring for human individuals and nurturing nature and thus would acknowledge the older generation of laborers. If sustaining families and communities were valued equally with producing goods, the care labor of women could be acknowledged as work.

Reconnection with the Shaowu community made me question whether factions could reunite despite all the separations and conflicts that resulted from privatization. After my full-year stay in 2013–14, I lived in Shaowu every other summer until the COVID-19 pandemic prevented travel. When I was away from them, I kept in touch with the sawmill community members mostly through online social networks. Although the retired workers are not affluent, they have much more time to relax, and several families often cook and eat meals together. These children of the migrants from northern China like to make dumplings and buns, and they often send me pictures and videos on WeChat showing them making food together and eating around a big round table. Just as they did after the ruptures in their work units, they are rebuilding the community. To recognize me as a member of the community, they send me these photos and tell me, "We all miss you so much. You should come back soon, so we can make dumplings and buns for you!"

NOTES

PREFACE

1. The song, called "Cong tou zai lai" in Chinese, was sung by Liu Huan.

2. The Chinese name of this sketch is *Da qi,* and the role of the male state worker was played by Huang Hong.

3. Examples of such cultural products include Li Tie's 2021 novel *Jin xiu,* which was heavily promoted by various government agencies and writers' associations; Luo Rixin's 2019 novella *Gang de cheng*; Zhang Meng's 2008 film *Erduo da you fu,* and the TV serial *Dongbei yijiaren,* directed by Ying Da, Lü Xiaopin, and Ying Ning (2001).

INTRODUCTION

1. The state logging camps (*famu chang*) in northern Fujian were renamed state forest farms (*caiyu chang* or *lin chang*) in the late 1970s in order to highlight their dual function: not only harvesting timber but also nurturing new trees. Their activities, however, did not change: they grew trees before the name change, and they continued logging after the renaming. The yield was consistent. But the name change reflects the emergence of an official discourse of preserving forests. In this book, I use *logging camp* to refer to these entities before about 1980 and *forest farm* thereafter, roughly corresponding to the Mao and post-Mao eras in China. In discussion spanning both eras, I use *forest farm,* a name that better captures the units' functions and does not erase women's work, which mostly consisted of nurturing trees.

2. Often translated as "(ecological) public welfare/benefit forests." See Robbins and Harrell, "Paradoxes and Challenges," and Liang, *Payment Schemes.*

3. Marx, *Grundrisse,* 191.

4. Other terms describing expropriation include *original accumulation* and *accumulation by dispossession.* Karl Marx coined the term *original accumulation* in vol. 1, chapter 26 of *Capital.* This term has also been translated as *primary accumulation* and *primitive accumulation.* At the core of Marx's concept of original accumulation is the process of "divorcing the producer from the means of production." This results in the

loss of people's essential means of social reproduction, thereby requiring them to sell their labor to those who now control the means of production. David Harvey explains the concept of "accumulation by dispossession" in "The 'New' Imperialism."

5. Meyskens, "Rethinking the Political Economy of Development."

6. Shapiro, *Mao's War against Nature.*

7. For details, see Wemheuer, *A Social History of Maoist China.*

8. Selden, *The Political Economy of Chinese Development.*

9. On the theorization and practices of primitive accumulation in the Soviet Union and China, see Preobrazhensky, "E. A. Preobrazhensky's Book 'Paper Money'"; Harrison, "Primary Accumulation"; Wen, *Zhongguo nongcun jiben jingji zhidu yanjiu* ; Day, *The Peasant*; Selden and Lippit, *The Transition to Socialism.*

10. See Li, Sato, and Sicular, *Rising Inequality*; Pun, *Migrant Labor.*

11. See Picketty, Yang, and Zucman, "Capital Accumulation."

12. Sheng, Song, and Yi, "Mechanisation Outsourcing"; Zhang, Oya, and Ye, "Bringing Agriculture Back In."

13. Nogueira, Guimarães, and Braga, "Inequalities and Capital Accumulation."

14. These projects include the Three-North Shelterbelt Programs (1978); the Greening Taihang Mountain Program (1987); the Desertification Control Program (1991); and the Natural Forest Preservation Program and the Returning Farmland to Forest Program (1999–2001).

15. Yong'an and Shaowu, both in Fujian, are both among the earliest pilot projects of forestry tenure reform in China. They completed the process of distributing forest usufruct to individual peasant households between 1998 and 2004. On June 25, 2003, the State Council of the PRC released the "Decision on Accelerating Forestry Development," which instituted strong protections for private tree ownership and the private wood market.

16. Naughton, *The Chinese Economy,* provides a chronological policy overview and interpretation for the socialist and post-1978 transitional economies.

17. In most places, provision of food was collective from 1956 on, while food processing and welfare were communalized only for short periods—about half a year in 1958, before famine struck and the collective canteens collapsed. For most of the collective years, the provision of food, clothing, shelter, and heating and the raising of children were left to households.

18. Meyskens, *Mao's Third Front.*

19. Mies, *Patriarchy and Accumulation*; Federici, *Caliban and the Witch*; Fortunati, *The Arcane of Reproduction.*

20. Harrison, "Primary Accumulation"; Wen, *Zhongguo nongcun jiben jingji zhidu yanjiu.*

21. The anthropologist Stevan Harrell divides the PRC's history into developmen-

talism (before 1998) and ecodevelopmentalism (following 1998). This ecosystemic approach is an alternative to the conventional periodization. See Harrell, *An Ecological History*.

22. Behar, *Translated Woman*; Gluck and Patai, *Women's Words*; Johnson, *Sweet Tea*; Barbre and Personal Narratives Group, *Interpreting Women's Lives*.

23. All personal names used in the book are pseudonymous to protect individuals' identities.

24. I attempted a few open-ended interviews with men at the beginning of my fieldwork, but they talked more about the changes in the industry and enterprise than about their personal lives and feelings. Therefore I use content from the men's interviews mainly to lay out the historical timeline and to explain technical aspects of forest farm and sawmill procedures.

25. In each chapter, when I talk about an interlocutor's life trajectory, specific events in this person's life, and her analysis of her work history and forestry development, this information comes from her life history interview. When I write about living and working conditions, as well as the impacts of reforms on women workers in the same group, I draw on narratives from other interviews as well. This approach allows me to present collective experiences and knowledge from that group of workers while using one life story to connect them.

26. Gail Hershatter, "Disquiet in the House of Gender."

ONE / MIGRATION FOR WORK IN FORESTRY

1. Quotations from Zhuang in this chapter are from my interviews with her on November 10 and 11, 2013. This chapter also draws on my interviews with former sawmill and forest farm workers between 2013 and 2018.

2. Chapter 1 of J. Brown, *City versus Countryside*, documents that the same happened in Tianjin.

3. Dorothy Solinger coined and defined this term in *Contesting Citizenship*. Nevertheless, access to benefits was not equal among the urban population. Some public goods were available only to state workers, not employees of the collective enterprises; some state employees received better treatment than their collective counterparts; and some work units had more public goods and benefits than others. See the discussion in Walder, "The Remaking of the Chinese Working Class," and Bian, *Work and Inequality*.

4. Knight and Song, *The Rural-Urban Divide*; Lardy, *Agriculture in China's Modern Economic Development*; Riskin, *China's Political Economy*; Sheng, *Intersectoral Resource Flows*.

5. For accounts of the Chinese iron and steel industry and technologies during the Great Leap Forward, see Wagner, "The Great Leap Forward."

6. Chapter 1 of J. Brown, *City versus Countryside*, examines the establishment and effects of the state grain monopoly in Tianjin and surrounding villages.

7. Richardson, *Forestry in Communist China*.

8. Li Jie, *Xinjiang nanjing diqu Hanzu yimin ji minzu guanxi yanjiu*; Hansen, *Frontier People*.

9. D. Liu, "Tenure and Management."

10. I follow James Scott in using this term to describe the hidden forms of resistance to oppression — the forms that are not openly declared and not recognized as typical "collective actions." See Scott, "Everyday Forms of Resistance."

11. The infrastructure of *danwei* is discussed in Bray, *Social Space and Governance*, 104, 142; Cao and Chu, *Urban Construction*, 52–54; Lü and Perry, *Danwei*; Dutton, *Streetlife China*.

12. Bray, *Social Space and Governance*, 93, 124, 150.

13. Lu, *Remaking Chinese Urban Form*, 47.

14. Lu, *Remaking Chinese Urban Form*, 70; Bray, *Social Space and Governance*, 143; Lü and Perry, *Danwei*, 42–59; Yang Dongping, *Chengshi jifeng*, 122.

15. Bray, *Social Space and Governance*, 249–58.

16. Walder, *Communist Neo-traditionalism*, 40–59.

17. Lu Duanfang captured a similar restriction in *Remaking Chinese Urban Form*, 53–58.

18. Chapter 7 of J. Brown, *City versus Countryside,* illustrates two similar examples. To take advantage of urban unemployment and the natural environment, two Tianjin work units were built in a rural area but designated as urban. The author argues that the frequent and hostile interactions between workers and peasants reinforced the rural/urban separation.

19. Knight and Song, *The Rural-Urban Divide*; Selden and Wu, "The Chinese State"; Eyferth, "Less for More."

20. Wen, *Zhongguo nongcun jiben jingji zhidu yanjiu*.

TWO / THE DEPENDENTS

1. The state logging camps in Fujian mostly planted two species of trees between the 1960s and 1980s: Chinese red pine (*Pinus massoniana*) and China fir (*Cunninghamia*). Fujianese who were familiar with the state logging camps often joked that their decades of work produced only two trees.

2. In the official documents, these workers were called "family dependents" (*jiashu*) and "family dependent workers" (*jiashu gong*), interchangeably. Generally, when considered as members of the dependents production team (*jiashu shengchan dui*), they were likely referred to as family dependent workers. Documents that mention other aspects of workers' lives often refer to them as dependents of their husbands. Workers in

the state forestry units use both terms to refer to themselves and peers. However, when dependent workers of the forest farms protested for their pensions, they strategically used the term *family dependent workers* to emphasize the fact that they worked for the forest farms and deserved pensions.

3. Quotations from Xiaomei and Laoniang in this chapter are from my interviews with them on April 18, 2014 and December 7, 2013, respectively. This chapter also draws on my interviews with other former forest farm and sawmill workers.

4. Wolf, *Revolution Postponed*.

5. Davin, *Woman-Work*. The work-point (*gong fen*) system was a method used during China's rural collectivization period to assess the quantity and quality of labor output and to determine the compensation received by the laborers.

6. Eyferth, "Less for More," "Women's Work," and *Eating Rice from Bamboo Roots*.

7. M. Brown, "Dutiful Help."

8. Song Shaopeng, "Cong zhangxian dao xiaoshi."

9. "Zhonghua quanguo zonggonghui zhaokai quanguo zhigong jiashu gongzuo huiyi."

10. Yang Zhihua, "Qinjian jianguo qinjian chijia wei shehui zhuyi jianshe gengda de Liliang."

11. In my study, the family dependent workers were mostly wives and occasionally older children of the male workers. But in some factories, especially those factories with a majority of female workers, like textile factories, women workers' mothers were recruited as dependent workers.

12. Yang Zhihua, "Qinjian jianguo qinjian chijia wei shehui zhuyi jianshe gengda de Liliang."

13. Lai Ruoyu, "Yingdang jiaqiang zhigong jiashu gongzuo."

14. Lai Ruoyu, "Guanche 'wuhao' qinjian chijia wei shehui zhuyi fuwu, quanguo zhigong jiashu daibiao huiyi kaimu."

15. "Niuzhuan zhegu niliu."

16. Song, "Cong zhangxian dao xiaoshi," 120.

17. Yang Zhihua, "Xuyan," in *Da yuejin zhong de zhigong jiashu*, 1–2.

18. "Cong 'guotai zhuan' dao "jiqi zhuan."

19. Wang Xiulan, "Zuohao jiashu gongzuo." in *Da yuejin zhong de zhigong jiashu*.

20. All-China Women's Federation Research Institute and Shanxi Women's Federation Research Center, *Zhongguo funü tongji ziliao 1949–1989*, 92, 239, 241.

21. Song, "Cong zhangxian dao xiaoshi," 121.

22. Friedrich Engels's *The Origin of the Family, Private Property, and the State* was one of the main ideological texts that informed the Chinese Communist Party's beliefs that bringing women into production played a crucial role in women's liberation. For Lenin's similar discussion, see *Liening quanji*, 1–26.

23. Song, "Cong zhangxian dao xiaoshi,"118.

24. All-China Women's Federation, "Wei xiezhu zhixing zhongyang renmin zhengfu zhengwuyuan guanyu laodong jiuye wenti de jueding gei geji fulian de tongzhi."

25. Song, "Cong zhangxian dao xiaoshi," 118.

26. Two prominent articles were published under the name Wan Muchun, which was very likely a pseudonym used by the central government to deliver its opinion. Song's article "Cong zhangxian dao xiaoshi," 123–24, discusses the political reasons for and results of these publications.

27. For detailed examples of how the CCP used the promise of helping men find wives, see Stacey, "China's Socialist Revolution"; K. Johnson, *Women, the Family, and Peasant Revolution*.

28. This was the expression that Xiaomei used in her interview. At that time, single men past their early twenties were considered "old bachelors" (*lao guang gun*).

29. Foot binding was a custom of tightly wrapping the feet of young girls. Intended to make the foot look small and delicate, it deformed the bones and made walking difficult. It was most popular between the Song and Qing dynasties.

30. Hershatter, *The Gender of Memory*.

31. For discussions of female employment in China, especially the ways female labor mobilization and demobilization were used during economic expansions and recessions, see Thorborg, "Chinese Employment Policy"; Jacka, *Women's Work*.

32. Marx, *Capital*, vol. 1, chapter 25.

33. For an analysis of how this perception has shaped women's employment around the world, starting in the 1970s, see Elson and Pearson, "'Nimble Fingers.'"

34. Wolf, *Revolution Postponed*.

35. A state factory running a farm by and for the workers was not an uncommon phenomenon. The Daqing Oilfield's model of "men industry, women agriculture" is discussed in Song Shaopeng, "Laohuizhan he daqing youtian."

36. Zachmann, "A Socialist Consumption Junction"; Oldenziel and Zachmann, *Cold War Kitchen*.

37. Malraux, *Anti-memoirs*.

38. Hershatter, *The Gender of Memory*.

39. Eyferth, "Less for More."

40. Marx, *Capital*, vol. 1, 667–80.

41. During the expansion of capitalism through colonialism, both colonizing countries and colonies exploited a supposedly natural connection between women and domestic and reproductive labor. For example, colonizers enabled craftswomen as producers and consumers but prohibited them from carrying out transactions or working outside the home without their husbands' permission. Meanwhile, they deprived

colonized women of the right to reproduce, literally not allowing enslaved women to marry or to have children, as it was cheaper to import new slaves than to fund the existing slaves' reproduction. See Mies, *Patriarchy and Accumulation*.

42. M. Brown, "Dutiful Help," 39–58.

43. This gender division intersected with other social categories. Not all women in the logging camps and sawmill were registered as dependents. Young women from Shanghai were categorized as state workers: they had a middle-school education and were considered intellectuals. Rural Shandongese female party members and cadres, like Zhuang Jinxian, were classified as state workers because of their demonstrated political loyalty. Widows who were sole the breadwinners in their households were classified as state workers as well. Thus the division between female state workers and female dependents intersected with marital status, geographic origin, and education. These various intersections were used to define some groups of women as exploitable reproductive labor both at home and in the public domain. Regardless of women's status, men were considered breadwinners.

THREE / ALIENATION

1. This chapter is based on interviews with forest farm workers, villagers, and south-western migrant workers conducted between 2014 and 2018.

2. Songster, "Cultivating the Nation"; Menzies, "A Survey of Customary Law and Control," 51; Macauley, *Social Power and Legal Culture*.

3. Songster, "Cultivating the Nation."

4. Coggins, "Ferns and Fire," 147, 146.

5. This provincial policy was guided by—yet differed from—the 1981 national policy of Three Fixes (*san ding*), which aimed to transfer property rights, benefits, and production responsibilities to peasant households by dividing up the collective forestland and establishing household ownership of forests. The central government terminated the Three Fixes policy between 1984 and 1985. The Central Committee of the Chinese Communist Party and the Chinese State Council's Resolution on Issues Concerning Forest Protection and Development, which initiated the policy, provided definitions and regulations governing *ziliu shan* and *ziren shan*. See Xu, "Collective Forest Tenure Reform in China"; Liang, *Payment Schemes*, 98–100.

6. Other studies show that rural households did not use the forests as a major source of revenue. See, for example, Xu, "Collective Forest Tenure Reform in China," 6. This Fujian-based study shows that forestry's contribution to rural income was negligible despite forestland's constituting over 60 percent of the province.

7. Coggins and Minor, "Fengshui Forests."

8. This decision was announced by the Central Committee of the Chinese Com-

munist Party and the State Council in "Guanyu jinyibu huoyue nongcun jingji de shixiang zhengce" on January 1, 1985. In the face of a nationwide surge of excessive and illegal logging, the Central Committee reversed itself and reinstated the local forestry bureaus' monopolistic control over the timber trade in 1987. However, the Fujian Provincial Forestry Department did not completely stop the collective timber trade but instead used the state sawmill as a trade coordinator. For details, see Liang, *Payment Schemes*, 55; Xu, "Collective Forest Tenure Reform in China," 4–5.

9. Robbins and Harrell, "Paradoxes and Challenges," 384, provides a table showing the changes in forested area and standing biomass in China from 1949 to 2008. It illustrates a big increase in forested area between 1973 and 1976 and a decrease between 1977 and 1981, followed by a consistent increase after 1984. Data from before the 1970s, however, are unreliable and controversial.

10. Ling, "Woguo senlin ziyuan de bianqian"; Songster, "Cultivating the Nation," 452–73; Menzies, "A Survey of Customary Law and Control," 51.

11. Rozelle et al., *China from Afforestation to Poverty Alleviation* 15–16, 19.

12. Liang, *Payment Schemes*, 3.

13. For recent research casting doubt on upstream deforestation as the cause of the 1998 mid-Changjiang area floods, see Schmidt et al., "The Question of Communist Land Degradation," 1–20.

14. Zong and Chen, "The 1998 Flood," 165–66.

15. Robbins and Harrell, "Paradoxes and Challenges," elaborates on these changes.

16. Chai, "Collective Forest Tenure Reform in Fujian," cited in Xu, "Collective Forest Tenure Reform in China," 2.

17. Urbanization, road access, and risk-management effects all contributed to an increase in off-farm jobs in China. Adams et al., "Impacts of Large-Scale Forest Restoration," 738.

18. Liang, *Payment Schemes*, 59. Classification-based forest management, mentioned in official documents in the early 1980s and mid-1990s, became government policy.

19. The central government's system of compensating owners and managers of ecological public benefit forestland was established in 2004. But the system was not fully instituted in Fujian until 2007, when the national funds were matched with Fujian provincial government funds and payment from the downstream regions in the province.

20. The impact of rural flight to the forests is discussed in Adams et al., "Impacts of Large-Scale Forest Restoration," 738. A survey conducted in another Fujianese village indicated that the residents thought soil erosion had been reduced. This survey's findings are also discussed in Liang, *Payment Schemes*, 84.

1. Lina's words quoted in this chapter are from my interviews with her on March 28 and April 20, 2014. I conducted an interview with Bao Yixiong on October 21, 2013.

2. The quote is from a directive written by Mao Zedong and published in the party newspaper *Renmin ribao* (People's Daily) on December 22, 1968. On the ways sent-down youths and local officials used resources that were made available through the movement in order to improve rural life and promote rural industry, see Honig and Zhao, "Sent-Down Youth and Rural Economic Development."

3. This model is called *dingti* in some places.

4. Tang and Ma, "Evolution of Urban Collective Enterprises"; State Statistical Bureau, *China Statistical*, 1981.

5. In the late 1990s and early 2000s, two forms of urban arrangement gradually replaced the *danwei* as the basic unit of urban life in China: the *xiaoqu* (microdistrict) and *shequ* (community). The *xiaoqu* bears many similarities to the *danwei*. Both types of units provide community facilities and often green areas for the exclusive use of their residents. However, the *xiaoqu* accommodates residents from different workplaces and backgrounds and thus does not play the role of fostering social interactions within a work unit or cultivating workers' collective identity. The *shequ*, composed of several *xiaoqu*, is regulated by a residents' committee. The *shequ* can provide government-funded services to residents, such as garbage collection, eldercare services, and other human services. The *shequ* took over the role of the *danwei* in promoting mass mobilization, organizing collective activities, and ensuring compliance with government directives such as China's earlier one-child policy and, more recently, COVID prevention protocols. The employees of the residents' committee are semigovernmental officials under the supervision of the county's street offices. The *xiaoqu* and *shequ* were supposed to replace all the residential and administrative functions of the *danwei*. However, the transition was not easy for many former state-enterprise *danwei* residents. See Bray, *Social Space and Governance*, 183, 192; Lu, *Remaking Chinese Urban Form*, 64.

6. Liu Yingli, "Jinnian gaobie xiagang zhigong"; Garnaut, Song, and Yao, "Impact and Significance."

7. State Council Information Office of the People's Republic of China, "Zhongguo de laodong he shehui baozhang zhuangkuang baipishu." There is a well-known ditty describing the three mass mobilizations and demobilizations during the lives of the layoff generation. "Chairman Mao sent us to the countryside [*xiaxiang*] in the '70s, Chairman Deng sent us into business [*xiahai*] in the '80s, Chairman Jiang sent us to the private sector [*xiagang*]." See Hung and Chiu, "The Lost Generation."

8. Wang cites this figure in "Gender Employment and Women's Resistance," 61,

originally published in *Zhongguo funübao* (China Women's News), 12 June 1998. See also J. Liu, *Gender and Work*, 6.

9. Appleton et al., "Labor Retrenchment"; Dong and Putterman, "China's State-Owned Enterprises"; Lee, "Livelihood Struggles"; Jiang Yongping, "Shiji zhi jiao guanyu jieduan jiuye funü huijia de da taolun."

10. Appleton et al., "Labor Retrenchment"; Anagnost, "What Can Suzhi Tell Us?"

11. Lee, "Livelihood Struggles"; Liu, *Gender and Work*, 90; Leung and Wong, "The Emergence of a Community-Based Social Assistance Programme."; Solinger, "Labor Market Reform"; Won, "Withering Away," 73.

12. Honig and Hershatter, *Personal Voices*.

13. Wang, "Gender, Employment and Women's Resistance."

14. Zhou Shuxuan, "Danwei zhidu zhuanbian dui nüxing de yingxiang."

15. Dai, "Invisible Writing," 228; Yang, "Reemployment Stars;" Kong, "Melodrama for Change"; Won, "Withering Away," 82.

16. This ironic situation did not change after China adopted a freer financial market as a condition of joining the World Trade Organization. The government still supported the financial market without providing financial literacy education to the public. China saw repeated crises involving stock, property, and peer-to-peer (P2P) lending after 2000. Hundreds of millions of ordinary people, especially middle-aged working-class people, lost their savings. For more on the P2P crisis in 2019, see Jao, "China's Online P2P Lending Industry."

17. Yang, "The Crisis of Masculinity."

18. This sentiment parallels that of workers in Daqing, discussed by Hou in *Building for Oil*: the people who were sent to remote places to build up the country and then disregarded when it became capitalist.

19. After the privatization of the Shaowu Sawmill, some sawmill workers attempted to replace the previous *danwei* management system with a new system. They tried to arrange for residents to pay the utility and service fees to the subdistrict office (*jiedao banshichu*, one of the smaller administrative divisions of urban China, usually one level below the city level), so that the office would be responsible for cleaning, lighting, and other public needs. They also tried to arrange for one of the workers to clean the public areas and let her charge the other residents. Both attempts failed for a similar reason: some of the residents paid, but others didn't. After the layoffs, many workers had to migrate to other cities for jobs, and many of them argued that since they worked and lived in another city for most of the year, it was unfair for them to have to pay every month. A few people thought the fees were too high. It was hard for these two thousand residents to figure out a new way of organizing and paying for public services that they had previously seen as free.

1. I translate *ku* as "bitter"; however, *ku* has broader meanings, including "pain," "suffering," and "unhappiness."

2. Li Lifeng, "Jingji de tugai yu zhengzhi de tugai," estimates that landlords owned 20 percent of the land in northern China, while middle peasants owned 50 percent. His estimation is based on Zhang Youyi, "Benshiji ersanshi niandai woguo diquan fenpei de zaiguji"; Wu Tingyu et al., *Xiandai Zhongguo nongcun jingji de yanbian*; Yuan and Dong, *Jindai Zhongguo xiaonong jingji de bianqian*.

3. Hinton, *Fanshen*, 157.

4. Huang, "Rural Class Struggle."

5. Li Lifeng, "Tugai zhong de suku."

6. Rofel, *Other Modernities*,140.

7. This document, titled "Shaowu Sawmill's Report on the Organizing Work of the Family Dependent Production Team," was addressed to the Fujian Provincial Forestry Department. The archive number is (66) Shaowu Sawmill, Labor, issue no. 028.

8. Mao used the word *fajue*, which means "to search and dig out," usually in the context of archeology and mining. Though it may not have been intentional, Mao's use of this word drew an analogy between women's labor power and a natural resource.

9. The Chinese term used in the document is *jiashu funü*, which translates literally as "family dependent women." I translate it as "dependent workers" here to maintain consistency of usage between chapters, as well as to emphasize the fact that almost all these women worked in the sawmill.

10. Bakken, *The Exemplary Society*.

11. Quotations from Waipo in this chapter come from my interview with her on August 20, 2011. This chapter also draws on my interviews with my mother, uncle, and other family members in 2011 and 2012.

12. See M. Brown, "Dutiful Help," on the long history of Chinese women's work that was not counted as labor (*laodong*).

13. Huang, *The Peasant Economy* and *The Peasant Family and Rural Development*.

14. Huang, *The Peasant Economy*; Crook and Crook, *Revolution in a Chinese Village*, 19–26; Hinton, *Fanshen*, 592; Wou, *Mobilizing the Masses*, 291–303.

15. Dunn, *Privatizing Poland*.

16. The Chinese title of this document is "Guanyu qiye zhigong yanglao baoxian zhidu gaige de jueding."

17. The Chinese title of this law is "Zhonghua Renmin Gongheguo laodongfa."

18. Merry, *Getting Justice*; Yngvesson, *Virtuous Citizens*.

19. Merry, *Getting Justice*.

20. Perry, "Chinese Conceptions of Rights."

21. Rofel, *Other Modernities*. Rofel observed how bitterly the oldest cohort of female workers at a state-owned textile mill (equal in status to forestry family dependent workers) spoke in their formal and informal comments in the 1980s. Even though the younger workers in the same community disliked these "complaints," the older women, still longing for recognition, continued to speak about the sufferings that, from their perspective, had a heroic quality.

22. Park, "Nongjiale Tourism"; Hubbert, "(Re)collecting Mao."

SIX / ADAPTING TACTICS

1. This chapter is primarily based on my interviews with former sawmill workers between 2014 and 2020 and my participant observation during their protests and campaign meetings in 2014.

2. Similar kinds of self-categorization are common in social movements. For example, although people who migrated from Asia to the United States might have similar experiences of immigration, employment, social interactions, and so on, not all Asians necessarily self-identify as Asian Americans. They might distance themselves from this collective definition for social, political, or pragmatic reasons.

3. It is not uncommon to see legal institutions create double jeopardies for marginalized groups. One case that made history in US employment law and the feminist movement was the 1976 lawsuit *DeGraffenreid v. General Motors Assembly Division, St. Louis*, in which five laid-off Black women from Missouri filed a class-action Title VII lawsuit against their former employer. But Title VII of the Civil Rights Act of 1964 failed to recognize the claims made by people who were discriminated against because of their intersectional identity—in this case, being Black and women. See Crenshaw, "Mapping the Margins," 1241. For more analysis of how the state and its laws compound the marginalization of people who occupy multiple disadvantaged social categories, see Nash, "Re-thinking Intersectionality"; Collins and Bilge, *Intersectionality*; Collins, "Intersectionality's Definitional Dilemmas"; King, "Multiple Jeopardy."

4. Jiang Zeming, "Jiang Zeming Lun Yushi Jujin."

5. O'Brien and Li, *Rightful Resistance*.

6. Jiangang Zhu, "Not against the State."

7. Woodman, "Law, Translation, and Voice."

8. Lorde, *The Master's Tools*.

9. On this phenomenon in the US Third World feminist movement, see Sandoval, *Methodology of the Oppressed*.

10. He, "Corruption and Anti-corruption."

11. Deng and O'Brien, "Societies of Senior Citizens."

12. Ai, *Taishi Village.*

13. Gallagher, "Mobilizing the Law."

EPILOGUE

1. Here are only a few examples of narratives about Chinese workers stealing American jobs: Porter, "On Trade, Angry Voters Have a Point"; Bartash, "China Really Is to Blame"; "Full Transcript: Donald Trump's Jobs Plan Speech." On Western leftists' attention to Chinese workers' resistance, especially strikes, in export-oriented factories, see "China's Growing Labour Movement"; Hurst, "Chinese Labor Divided"; Ren, Fan, and Kosuth, "Class Struggle in China."

BIBLIOGRAPHY

Adams, Cristina, Sidney T. Rodrigues, Miguel Calmon, and Chetan Kumar. "Impacts of Large-Scale Forest Restoration on Socioeconomic Status and Local Livelihoods: What We Know and Do Not Know." *Biotropica* 48, no. 6 (2016): 731–44.

Ai Xiaoming. *Taishi Village.* DVD. Hong Kong: Universities Services Centre, 2005.

Alexander, M. Jacqui, and Chandra Talpade Mohanty. *Feminist Genealogies, Colonial Legacies, Democratic Futures.* New York: Routledge, 1997.

All-China Federation of Trade Union's Women Worker Council and All-China Women's Federation's Propaganda Office. *Da Yuejin zhong de zhigong jiashu* (Dependents in the Great Leap Forward). Beijing: Gongren Chubanshe, 1960.

All-China Women's Federation. "Wei xiezhu zhongyang renmin zhengfu zhengwuyuan guanyu laodong jiuye wenti de jueding gei geji Fulian de tongzhi" (Notification to all Women's Federation branches in order to assist in implementing the central government's directive on employment). *Renmin ribao*, August 10, 1952.

All-China Women's Federation Research Institute and Shanxi Women's Federation Research Center. *Zhongguo funü tonji ziliao 1949–1989* (Chinese women's statistics, 1949–1989). Beijing: Zhongguo Tongji Chubanshe, 1991.

Anagnost, Ann. "What Can Suzhi Tell Us about the Global Economy? Embodiments of Value in China's Economic Reform." Lecture delivered at the University of Warwick. May 20, 2017.

Appleton, Simon, John Knight, Lina Song, and Qingjie Xia. "Labor Retrenchment in China: Determinants and Consequences." *China Economic Review* 13, no. 2 (2002): 252–75.

Bakken, Børge. *The Exemplary Society: Human Improvement, Social Control, and the Dangers of Modernity in China.* Oxford: Oxford University Press, 2000.

Barbre, Joy Webster, and Personal Narratives Group. *Interpreting Women's Lives: Feminist Theory and Personal Narratives.* Bloomington: Indiana University Press, 1989.

Bartash, Jeffry. "China Really Is to Blame for Millions of Lost U.S. Manufacturing Jobs, New Study Finds." MarketWatch. May 14, 2017. www.marketwatch.com/story/china-really-is-to-blame-for-millions-of-lost-us-manufacturing-jobs-new-study-finds-2018-05-14.

Behar, Ruth. *Translated Woman: Crossing the Border with Esperanza's Story*. Boston: Beacon Press, 1993.

Bhattacharya, Tithi, and Lise Vogel. *Social Reproduction Theory: Remapping Class, Recentering Oppression*. London: Pluto, 2017.

Bian, Yanjie. *Work and Inequality in Urban China*. Albany: State University of New York Press, 1994.

Bray, David. *Social Space and Governance in Urban China: The* Danwei *System from Origins to Reform*. Stanford, CA: Stanford University Press, 2005.

Brown, Jeremy. *City versus Countryside in Mao's China: Negotiating the Divide*. New York: Cambridge University Press, 2012.

Brown, Melissa. "Dutiful Help: Masking Rural Women's Economic Contributions." In *Transforming Patriarchy: Chinese Families in the Twenty-first Century*, edited by Gonçalo Santos and Stevan Harrell, 39–58. Seattle: University of Washington Press, 2017.

Cao, Hongtao, and Chuanheng Chu. *Urban Construction in Contemporary China*. Beijing: China Social Science Press, 1990.

Central Committee of the Chinese Communist Party and Chinese State Council. *Guanyu baohu senlin fazhan linye ruogan wenti de jueding* (Resolution on issues concerning forest protection and development). March 1981.

———. *Guanyu jinyibu huoyue nongcun jingji de shixiang zhengce* (Ten policies to further activate the rural economy). January 1, 1985.

Chai, Xitang. "Collective Forest Tenure Reform in Fujian." Presentation at International Workshop on Forest Tenure Reform, Beijing, September 21, 2006.

"China's Growing Labour Movement Offers Hope for Workers Globally." The Conversation. April 16, 2015. https://theconversation.com/chinas-growing-labour-movement-offers-hope-for-workers-globally-39921.

Coggins, Chris. "Ferns and Fire: Village Subsistence, Landscape Change, and Nature Conservation in China's Southeast Uplands." *Journal of Cultural Geography* 19, no. 2 (2002): 12–159.

Coggins, Chris, and Jesse Minor. "Fengshui Forests as A Socio-natural Reservoir in the Face of Climate Change and Environmental Transformation." *Asia Pacific Perspectives* 15, no. 2 (2018): 4–29.

Collins, Patricia Hill. *Black Feminist Thought: Knowledge, Consciousness, and the Politics of Empowerment*. 2nd ed. New York: Routledge, 2009.

———. "Intersectionality's Definitional Dilemmas." *Annual Review of Sociology* 41, no. 1 (2015): 1–20.

Collins, Patricia Hill, and Sirma Bilge. *Intersectionality (Key Concepts)*. Cambridge: Polity Press, 2016.

"Cong 'guotai zhuan' dao 'jiqi zhuan': Gao Fengqin tan yige gongchang zhigong jiashu de dayuejin." (From 'turning the pot' to 'turning the machine': Representative Gao Fengqin addresses the Great Leap Forward of a dependent). *Renmin ribao*, April 30, 1959.

Crenshaw, Kimberlé. "Mapping the Margins: Intersectionality, Identity Politics, and Violence against Women of Color." *Stanford Law Review* 43, no. 6 (1991): 1241–99.

Crook, Isabel, and Crook, David. *Revolution in a Chinese Village, Ten Mile Inn*. London: Routledge and Kegan Paul, 1959.

Croll, Elisabeth. *Chinese Women since Mao*. London: Zed Books, 1983.

Dahl, Hanne Marlene, Rasmus Willig, and Pauline Stoltz. "Recognition, Redistribution and Representation in Capitalist Global Society: An Interview with Nancy Fraser." *Acta Sociologica* 47, no. 4 (2004): 374–82.

Dai, Jinhua. "Class and Gender in Contemporary Chinese Women's Literature." In *Holding Up Half the Sky: Chinese Women Past, Present, and Future*, edited by Jie Tao, Bijun Zheng, and Shirley Mow, 289–301. New York: Feminist Press at the City University of New York, 2004.

———. "Daoyan er: liangnan zhijian huo tuwei keng?" (Introduction 2: Between two dilemmas, or a chance to break out?) In *Funü, minzu yu nüxing zhuyi* (Women, nation, and feminism), edited by Chen Shunxin, 27–38. Zhongguo Bianyi Chubanshe, 2004.

———. "Invisible Writing: The Politics of Mass Culture in the 1990s." In *Cinema and Desire: Feminist Marxism and Cultural Politics in the Work of Dai Jinhua*, edited by Jing Wang and Tani E. Barlow, 213–34. London: Verso, 2002.

Davin, Delia. *Woman-Work: Women and the Party in Revolutionary China*. Oxford: Oxford University Press, 1979.

Day, Alexander. *The Peasant in Postsocialist China: History, Politics, and Capitalism*. Cambridge: Cambridge University Press, 2013.

Deng, Yanhua, and Kevin J. O'Brien. "Societies of Senior Citizens and Popular Protest in Rural Zhejiang." *China Journal* 71, no. 1 (2014): 172–88.

Dong, Xiao-Yuan, and Louis Putterman. "China's State-Owned Enterprises in the First Reform Decade: An Analysis of a Declining Monopsony." *Economics of Planning* 35, no. 2 (2002): 109–39.

Dörre, Klaus, Stephan Lessenich, and Rosa Hartmut. *Sociology, Capitalism, Critique*. Translated by Loren Balhorn and Jan-Peter Herrmann. London: Verso, 2015.

Dunn, Elizabeth. *Privatizing Poland: Baby Food, Big Business, and the Remaking of Labor*. Ithaca, NY: Cornell University Press, 2004.

Dutton, Michael Robert. *Streetlife China*. Cambridge: Cambridge University Press, 1998.

Elson, Diane, and Ruth Pearson. "'Nimble Fingers Make Cheap Workers': An Analysis of Women's Employment in Third World Export Manufacturing." *Feminist Review*, no. 7 (Spring 1981): 87–107.

Engels, Friedrich. *The Origin of the Family, Private Property, and the State.* New York: International Publishers, 1942.

Ewick, Patricia, and Susan S. Silbey. "A Diversity of Influence: Conformity, Contestation, and Resistance; An Account of Legal Consciousness." *New England Law Review* 26 (1992): 731–49.

Eyferth, Jacob. *Eating Rice from Bamboo Roots: The Social History of a Community of Handicraft Papermakers in Rural Sichuan, 1920–2000.* Cambridge, MA: Harvard University Asia Center, 2009.

———. "Less for More: Rural Women's Overwork and Underconsumption in Mao's China." *Clio* 41 (2015): 65–84.

———. "Women's Work and the Politics of Homespun in Socialist China, 1949–1980." *International Review of Social History* 57, no. 3 (2012): 365–91.

Federici, Silvia. *Caliban and the Witch: Women, the Body and Primitive Accumulation.* 2nd rev. ed. Brooklyn, NY: Autonomedia, 2014.

———. *Revolution at Point Zero: Housework, Reproduction, and Feminist Struggle.* Oakland, CA: PM Press, 2012.

Fortunati, Leopoldina. *The Arcane of Reproduction: Housework, Prostitution, Labor and Capital.* New York: Autonomedia, 1996.

Fraser, Nancy. "Expropriation and Exploitation in Racialized Capitalism: A Reply to Michael Dawson." *Critical Historical Studies* 3, no. 1 (2016): 163–78.

———. "From Redistribution to Recognition? Dilemmas of Justice in a 'Post-socialist' Age." *New Left Review* 212 (July–August 1995): 68–93.

"Full Transcript: Donald Trump's Jobs Plan Speech." Politico. June 28, 2016. www .politico.com/story/2016/06/full-transcript-trump-job-plan-speech-224891.

Gallagher, Mary. "Mobilizing the Law in China: 'Informed Disenchantment' and the Development of Legal Consciousness." *Law and Society Review* 40, no. 4 (2006): 783–816.

Garnaut, Ross, Ligang Song, and Yang Yao. "Impact and Significance of State-Owned Enterprise Restructuring." *China Journal* 55 (2006):35–65.

Gluck, Sherna Berger, and Daphne Patai. *Women's Words: The Feminist Practice of Oral History.* New York: Routledge, 1991.

Gonçalves, Guilherme Leite, and Sérgio Costa. "From Primitive Accumulation to Entangled Accumulation: Decentring Marxist Theory of Capitalist Expansion." *European Journal of Social Theory* 23, no. 2 (May 2020): 146–64. https://doi.org/10.1177 /1368431018825064.

Hansen, Mette Halskov. *Frontier People: Han Settlers in Minority Areas of China.* Vancouver: UBC Press, 2005.

Harrell, Stevan. *An Ecological History of Modern China*. Seattle: University of Washington Press, 2023.

———. "From 'Humanity is Destined to Conquer Nature' to 'Building an Ecological Civilization': Development, Revolution, and Science in the Ideology of the Chinese Communist Party." Presentation at Greater China Environment Workshop, Tacoma, April 2019.

Harrison, Mark. "Primary Accumulation in the Soviet Transition." *Journal of Development Studies* 22, no. 1 (1985): 81–103.

Harvey, David. "The 'New' Imperialism: Accumulation by Dispossession." In *Socialist Register 2004: The New Imperial Challenge*, vol. 40, edited by Leo Panitch and Colin Leys, 63–87. 2009. https://socialistregister.com/index.php/srv/article/view/5811.

He, Zengke. "Corruption and Anti-corruption in Reform China." *Communist and Post-Communist Studies* 33, no. 2 (2000): 243–70.

Hershatter, Gail. "Disquiet in the House of Gender." *Journal of Asian Studies* 71, no. 4 (2012): 873–94.

———. *The Gender of Memory*. Berkeley: University of California Press, 2011.

Hinton, William. *Fanshen: A Documentary of Revolution in a Chinese Village*. Berkeley: University of California Press, 1966.

Honig, Emily, and Gail Hershatter. *Personal Voices: Chinese Women in the 1980s*. Stanford, CA: Stanford University Press, 1988.

Honig, Emily, and Xiaojian Zhao. "Sent-Down Youth and Rural Economic Development in Maoist China." *China Quarterly* 222 (2015): 499–521.

Hou, Li. *Building for Oil: Daqing and the Formation of the Chinese Socialist State*. Cambridge, MA: Harvard University Asia Center, 2018.

Huang, Philip C. *The Peasant Economy and Social Change in North China*. Stanford, CA: Stanford University Press, 1985.

———. *The Peasant Family and Rural Development in the Yangzi Delta, 1350–1988*. Stanford, CA: Stanford University Press, 1990.

———. "Rural Class Struggle in the Chinese Revolution: Representational and Objective Realities from the Land Reform to the Cultural Revolution." *Modern China* 21, no. 1 (1995): 105–43.

Hubbert, Jennifer. "(Re)collecting Mao: Memory and Fetish in Contemporary China." *American Ethnologist* 33, no. 2 (2006): 145–61.

Hung, Eva P. W., and Stephen W. K. Chiu. "The Lost Generation: Life Course Dynamics and Xiagang in China." *Modern China* no. 2, vol 29 (2003): 204–36.

Hurst, William. "Chinese Labor Divided." Dissent Magazine. Spring 2015. www.dissentmagazine.org/article/chinese-labor-divided.

Jacka, Tamara. *Women's Work in Rural China: Change and Continuity in an Era of Reform*. Cambridge: Cambridge University Press, 1997.

Jao, Nicole. "China's Online P2P Lending Industry is Undergoing a Massive Shake Out." *Technode*, February 21, 2019. https://technode.com/2019/02/21/chinas-online -p2p-lending-industry-is-undergoing-of-a-massive-shake-out.

Jiang Yongping. "Shiji zhijiao guanyu 'jieduan jiuye' 'funü huijia' de da taolun" (The debate over "staged employment" and "women's returning home" at the turn of the century). *Funü yanjiu luncong* (Journal of Chinese Women's Studies), no. 2 (2001): 23–28.

Jiang Zeming. "Jiang Zeming Lun 'Yushi Jujin'" (Jiang Zeming's analysis of "To Advance with the Times"). Zhonggong Zhongyang Dangshi he Wenxian Yanjiu Yuan, July 12, 2012. www.dswxyjy.org.cn/n1/2019/0228/c425426-30909747.html.

Johnson, E. Patrick. *Sweet Tea: Black Gay Men of the South*. Chapel Hill: University of North Carolina Press, 2008.

Johnson, Kay Ann. *Women, the Family, and Peasant Revolution in China*. Chicago: University of Chicago Press, 1983.

King, Deborah. "Multiple Jeopardy, Multiple Consciousness: The Context of a Black Feminist Ideology." *Signs* 14, no. 1 (1988): 42–72.

Knight, John, and Lina Song. *The Rural-Urban Divide: Economic Disparities and Interactions in China*. Oxford: Oxford University Press, 1999.

Kong, Shuyu. "Melodrama for Change: Gender, Kuqing Xi and The Affective Articulation of Chinese TV Drama." In *Political Economy of Affect and Emotion in East Asia*, edited by Jie Yang, 116–34. London: Routledge, 2004.

Lai Ruoyu. "Guanche 'Wuhao' qinjian chijia wei shehui zhuyi fuwu, quanguo zhigong jiashu daibiao huiyi kaimu" (Implementing Five Goods, thrifty for the family and for socialism). *Renmin ribao*, June 5, 1957.

———. "Yingdang jiaqiang zhigong jiashu gongzuo" (Strengthening the work on dependents)." *Gongren ribao*, June 3, 1957.

Lardy, Nicholas. *Agriculture in China's Modern Economic Development*. Cambridge: Cambridge University Press, 1983.

Lee, Ching Kwan. "*Livelihood Struggles and Market Reform: (Un)marking Chinese Labor after State Socialism*. United Nations Research Institute for Social Development. February 2005. www.unrisd.org/unrisd/website/document.nsf/(httpPublications) /755EB01A0C1A165BC125700E00380454?OpenDocument.

Lenin, Vladimir. *Liening quanji*. (Collected works of Lenin). Translated by Zhonggong Zhongyang makesi engesi liening sidalin zhuzuo bianyiju (Chinese Communist Party–Central Government's Marx-Engels-Lenin-Stalin Translation Department). Beijing: Renmin Chubanshe, 1986.

Leung, J. C. B., and H. S. W. Wong. "The Emergence of a Community-Based Social Assistance Programme in Urban China." *Social Policy and Administration* 33, no. 1 (1999): 39–54.

Li Jie. *Xinjiang nanjiang diqu Hanzu yimin ji minzu guanxi yanjiu* (A study of Han migrants in southern Xinjiang and interethnic relations). Beijing: Minzu Chubanshe, 2010.

Li, Lifeng. "Economically-Oriented Land Reform vs. Politically-Oriented Land Reform: Rethinking Its Historical Significance" (Jingji de tugai yu zhengzhi de tugai—guanyu tudi gaige lishi yiyi de zaisikao). *Anhui shixue*, no. 2 (2008): 68–80 [in Chinese].

———. "Tugai zhong de suku: yizhong minzhong dongyuan jishu de weiguan fenxi" (Speaking bitterness in the Land Reform Movement: A microanalysis of an effective technique of mobilizing the masses). *Nanjing daxue xuebao* no. 5 (2007): 97–109.

Li, Shi, Hiroshi Sato, and Terry Sicular. *Rising Inequality in China: Challenges to a Harmonious Society*. Cambridge: Cambridge University Press, 2015.

Li Tie. "Jin Xiu" (The splendid). *Zhongguo zuojia* (Chinese writers). July 2021.

Liang, Dan. *Payment Schemes for Forest Ecosystem Services in China: Policy, Practices and Performance*. Wageningen: Wageningen Academic Publishers, 2012.

Ling Daxie. "Woguo senlin ziyuan de bianqian" (Changes in Chinese forest resources), *Zhongguo nongshi* (Chinese agricultural history) no. 2 (1983): 26–36.

Liu, Dachang. "Tenure and Management of Non-state Forests in China since 1950: A Historical Review." *Environmental History* 6, no. 2 (2001): 239–63.

Liu, Jieyu. *Gender and Work in Urban China: Women Workers of the Unlucky Generation*. London: Routledge, 2007.

Liu, Lydia He, Rebecca Karl, and Dorothy Ko. *The Birth of Chinese Feminism: Essential Texts in Transnational Theory*. New York: Columbia University Press, 2013.

Liu Yingli. "Jinnian gaobie xiagang zhigong" (Bidding farewell to this year's laid-off workers). *Zhongguo xinwen zhoukan*, 220, March 1, 2005.

Lorde, Audre. *The Master's Tools Will Never Dismantle the Master's House*. London: Penguin Modern, 2018.

Lu, Duanfang. *Remaking Chinese Urban Form: Modernity, Scarcity and Space, 1949–2005*. London: Routledge, 2006.

Lü, Xiaobo, and Elizabeth J. Perry. *Danwei: The Changing Chinese Workplace in Historical and Comparative Perspective*. Armonk, NY: M. E. Sharpe, 1997.

Luo Rixin. *Gang de cheng* (The city of steel). Renmin Wenxue Chubanshe. 2022.

Luxemburg, Rosa. *The Accumulation of Capital*. London: Routledge, 2003.

Macauley, Melissa. *Social Power and Legal Culture: Litigation Masters in Late Imperial China*. Stanford, CA: Stanford University Press, 1998.

Malraux, André. *Anti-memoirs*. New York: Bantam, 1970.

Mao Zedong. *Selected Works of Mao Tse-Tung*. 1st ed. Oxford: Pergamon, 1961.

Marx, Karl. *Capital: A Critique of Political Economy*. 3 vols. New York: International Publishers, 1967.

———. *Critique of the Gotha Programme*. Cabin John, MD: Wildside Press, 2008.

———. *Grundrisse: Foundations of the Critique of Political Economy*. London: Penguin, 2005.

McCann, Michael, and Tracey March. "Law and Everyday Forms of Resistance: A Socio-political Assessment." *Studies in Law, Politics, and Society* 15, no. 1 (1995): 207–36.

Menzies, Nicholas. "A Survey of Customary Law and Control over Trees and the Wildlands in China." In *Whose Trees? Proprietary Dimensions of Forestry*, edited by Louise Fortmann and John Bruce, 51–62. Boulder: Westview, 1988.

Merry, Sally Engle. *Getting Justice and Getting Even: Legal Consciousness among Working-Class Americans*. Chicago: University of Chicago Press, 1990.

Meyskens, Covell F. 2020. *Mao's Third Front: the Militarization of Cold War China*. Cambridge: Cambridge University Press.

———. "Rethinking the Political Economy of Development in Mao's China." *Positions: East Asia Cultures Critique* 29, no. 4 (2021): 809–34.

Mies, Maria. *Patriarchy and Accumulation on a World Scale: Women in the International Division of Labour*. 3rd ed. London: Zed Books, 2014.

Mohanty, Chandra Talpade. "Under Western Eyes: Feminist Scholarship and Colonial Discourses." *Boundary 2* 12, no. 3 (1984): 333–58.

Moya, Paula. *Learning from Experience: Minority Identities, Multicultural Struggles*. Berkeley: University of California Press, 2002.

Nader, Laura, Alicia Barabas, Miguel Bartolome, John Bodley, Guita Debert, Susan Drucker-Brown, Hugh Gusterson, Ellen Hertz, Margaret Lock, June Nash, and Rik Pinxten. "Controlling Processes: Tracing the Dynamic Components of Power." *Current Anthropology* 38, no. 5 (1997): 711–37.

Nash, Jennifer. "Re-thinking Intersectionality." *Feminist Review* no. 89 (2008): 1–15.

Naughton, Barry. *The Chinese Economy: Adaptation and Growth*. 2nd ed. Cambridge, MA: MIT Press, 2018.

"Niuzhuan zhegu niliu" (Turn back the countercurrent). *Renmin ribao*, September 6, 1957.

Nogueira, Isabela, João Victor Guimarães, and João Pedro Braga. "Inequalities and Capital Accumulation in China." *Brazilian Journal of Political Economy* 39, no. 3 (2019): 449–69.

O'Brien, Kevin, and Lianjiang Li. *Rightful Resistance in Rural China*. Cambridge: Cambridge University Press, 2006.

Oldenziel, Ruth, and Karin Zachmann. *Cold War Kitchen: Americanization, Technology and European Users*. Cambridge, MA: MIT Press, 2009.

Park, Choong-Hwan. "Nongjiale Tourism and Contested Space in Rural China." *Modern China* 40, no. 5 (2014): 519–48.

Perry, Elizabeth. "Chinese Conceptions of Rights: From Mencius to Mao and Now." *Perspectives on Politics* 6, no. 1 (2008): 37–50.

Piketty, Thomas, Li Yang, and Gabriel Zucman. "Capital Accumulation, Private Property, and Rising Inequality in China, 1978–2015." *American Economic Review*, 109, no. 7 (2019): 2469–96.

Porter, Eduardo. "On Trade, Angry Voters Have a Point." *New York Times*, March 15, 2016.

Preobrazhensky, Yevgeni. "E. A. Preobrazhensky's Book 'Paper Money in The Epoch of Proletarian Dictatorship, 1920.'" In *The Preobrazhensky Papers*, translated and edited by Richard B. Day and Mikhail M. Gorinov. Leiden, The Netherlands: Brill, 2014.

Pun, Ngai. *Migrant Labor in China: Post-socialist Transformations*. Malden, MA: Polity Press, 2016.

Ren, Hao, Fan Gang, and Dennis Kosuth. "Class Struggle in China." International Socialist Review. Fall 2016. https://isreview.org/issue/102/class-struggle-china.

Richardson, S. D. *Forestry in Communist China*. Baltimore, MD: Johns Hopkins Press, 1966.

Riskin, Carl. *China's Political Economy: The Quest for Development since 1949*. Oxford: Oxford University Press, 1987.

Robbins, Alicia S. T, and Stevan Harrell. "Paradoxes and Challenges for China's Forests in the Reform Era." *China Quarterly* 218, no. 1 (2014): 381–403.

Rodrik, Dani. "After Neoliberalism, What?" Presentation at BNDES Seminar on New Paths of Development, Rio de Janeiro, September 12–13, 2002.

Rofel, Lisa. *Other Modernities: Gendered Yearnings in China after Socialism*. Berkeley: University of California Press, 1999.

Rozelle, Scott, Jikun Huang, Syed Arif Husain, and Aaron Zazueta. *China from Afforestation to Poverty Alleviation and Natural Forest Management*. Washington, DC: World Bank, 2000.

Sandoval, Chela. *Methodology of the Oppressed*. Minneapolis: University of Minnesota Press, 2000.

Schmidt, Amanda, David R. Montgomery, Katharine W Huntington, and Chuan Liang. "The Question of Communist Land Degradation: New Evidence from Local Erosion and Basin-Wide Sediment Yield in Southwest China and Southeast Tibet." *Annals of the Association of American Geographers* 101, no. 3 (2011): 477–96.

Scott, James C. "Everyday Forms of Resistance." *Copenhagen Journal of Asian Studies* 4, no. 1 (1989): 33.

Selden, Mark. *The Political Economy of Chinese Development*. London: Routledge, 1994.

Selden, Mark, and Victor D. Lippit. *The Transition to Socialism in China*. Armonk, NY: M. E. Sharpe, 1982.

Selden, Mark, and Jieh-min Wu. "The Chinese State, Incomplete Proletarianization and Structures of Inequality in Two Epochs." *Asia-Pacific Journal* 9, no. 1 (2011): 1–23.

Shapiro, Judith. *Mao's War against Nature: Politics and the Environment in Revolutionary China*. Cambridge: Cambridge University Press, 2004.

Sheng, Yu, Ligang Song, and Qing Yi. "Mechanisation Outsourcing and Agricultural Productivity for Small Farms: Implications for Rural Land Reform in China." In *China's New Sources of Economic Growth*, 289–313. Edited by Ligang Song, Ross Garnaut, Cai Fang, and Laurne Johnston. Canberra: Australian National University Press.

Sheng, Yuming. *Intersectoral Resource Flows and China's Economic Development*. New York: St. Martin's, 1993.

Solinger, Dorothy. *Contesting Citizenship in Urban China: Peasant Migrants, the State, and the Logic of the Market*. Berkeley: University of California Press, 1999.

———. "Labour Market Reform and the Plight of the Laid-off Proletariat." *China Quarterly*, no. 170 (June 2002): 304–26.

Song Shaopeng. "Cong zhangxian dao xiaoshi: Jiti zhuyi shiqi de jiating laodong, 1949–1996" (From visible to invisible: Housework in the collectivist period) *Jiangsu shehui kexue* (Jiangsu Social Sciences) no. 1 (2012): 116–25.

———. "Laohuizhan he Daqing Youtian: Saertu de gushi" (Laohuizhan and the Daqing Oil Field: The story of Saertu). *Kaifang shidai* (Open Times), no. 3 (2012), 2.

Songster, Elena. "Cultivating the Nation in Fujian's Forests: Forest Policies and Afforestation Efforts in China, 1911–1937." *Environmental History* 8, no. 3 (2003): 452–73.

Spade, Dean. *Normal Life: Administrative Violence, Critical Trans Politics, and the Limits of Law*. Durham, NC: Duke University Press, 2015.

Stabile, Carol A., and Deepa Kumar. "Unveiling Imperialism: Media, Gender and the War on Afghanistan." *Media, Culture and Society* 27, no. 5 (2005): 765–82.

Stacey, Judith. "China's Socialist Revolution, Peasant Families, and the Uses of the Past." *Theory and Society* 9, no. 2 (1980): 269–81.

———. *Patriarchy and Socialist Revolution in China*. Berkeley: University of California Press, 1983.

State Council Information Office of the People's Republic of China. *Zhongguo de laodong he shehui baozhang zhuangkuang baipishu* (White paper on labor and social security in China). April 29, 2002.

State Statistical Bureau. *China Statistical*. Beijing: China Statistics Press, 1981.

Swarr, Amanda Lock, and Richa Nagar. "Dismantling Assumptions: Interrogating 'Lesbian' Struggles for Identity and Survival in India and South Africa." *Signs* 29, no. 2 (2004): 491–516.

Tang, Jianzhong, and Laurence J. C. Ma. "Evolution of Urban Collective Enterprises in China." *China Quarterly*, No. 104 (1985): 614–40.

Thorborg, Marina. "Chinese Employment Policy in 1949–1978, with Special Emphasis on Women in Rural Production." In *Chinese Economy Post-Mao: A Compendium of Papers Submitted to the Joint Economic Committee Congress of the United States*, vol. 1, *Policy and Performance*, edited by Robert Dernberger, Nicholas Lardy, and William Whitson, 538–601. Washington, DC: U.S. Government Printing Office, 1979.

Tian, Yiyu. "Trapped in Time: Bodily Experiences of Family Dependent Workers (*jiashu*) in Daqing, a Model Industrial City in High-Socialist China." MA thesis, University of Washington, 2019.

Trautner, Mary Nell. "Doing Gender, Doing Class: The Performance of Sexuality in Exotic Dance Clubs." *Gender and Society* 19, no. 6 (2005): 771–88.

Wagner, Donald. "The Great Leap Forward in Iron and Steel, 1958–60." http://don wagner.dk/MS-English/GreatLeap.html.

Walder, Andrew. *Communist Neo-traditionalism: Work and Authority in Chinese Industry*. Berkeley: University of California Press, 1986.

———. "The Remaking of the Chinese Working Class, 1949–1981." *Modern China* 10, no. 1 (1984): 3–48.

Wang Xiulan. "Zuohao jiashu gongzuo, zhiyuan gangtie shengchan" (Mobilizing dependents, supporting steel production). In *Da yuejin zhong de zhigong jiashu* (Dependents in the Great Leap Forward), edited by All-China Federation of Trade Unions Women Worker's Council and All-China Women's Federation'Propaganda Office, 10–11. Beijing: Gongren Chubanshe, 1960.

Wang, Zheng. *Finding Women in the State: A Socialist Feminist Revolution in the People's Republic of China, 1949–1964*. Oakland, CA: University of California Press, 2017.

———. "Gender, Employment and Women's Resistance." In *Chinese Society: Change, Conflict and Resistance*, edited by Elizabeth J. Perry and Mark Selden, 162–86. London: Routledge Curzon, 2003.

———. *Women in the Chinese Enlightenment: Oral and Textual Histories*. Berkeley, CA: University of California Press, 1999.

Weller, Robert P. *Discovering Nature Globalization and Environmental Culture in China and Taiwan*. Cambridge: Cambridge University Press, 2006.

Wemheuer, Felix. *A Social History of Maoist China: Conflict and Change, 1949–1976*. Cambridge: Cambridge University Press, 2019).

Wen Tiejun. *Zhongguo nongcun jiben jingji zhidu yanjiu: "Sannong" wenti de shiji fansi* (A study of the fundamental economic institutions of Chinese villages: A centennial reflection on the "Three Rurals" problem). Beijing: Zhongguo Jingji Chubanshe, 2000.

Wolf, Margery. *Revolution Postponed: Women in Contemporary China*. Stanford, CA: Stanford University Press, 1985.

Won, Jaeyoun. "Withering Away of the Iron Rice Bowl? The Reemployment Project of Post-socialist China." *Studies in Comparative International Development* 39, no. 2 (2004): 71–93.

Woodman, Sophia. "Law, Translation, and Voice." *Critical Asian Studies* 43, no. 2 (2011): 185–210.

Wou, Odoric Y. K. *Mobilizing the Masses: Building Revolution in Henan.* Stanford, CA: Stanford University Press, 1994.

Wu, Tingyu, Chen Yufeng, and Zhang Zhanbin. *Xiandai Zhongguo nongcun jingji de yanbian* (The transformation of the rural economy in Modern China). Changchun: Jinlin Renmin Chubanshe, 1993.

Xu, Jintao. "Collective Forest Tenure Reform in China: What Has Been Achieved So Far?" Initiative for Policy Dialogue. 2008. http://policydialogue.org/files/events /XuJintao_collective_forest_tenure_reform_china.pdf.

Yang Dongping. *Chengshi jifeng: Beijing he Shanghai de wenhua jingshen* (Urban monsoon: The cultural spirit of Beijing and Shanghai). Beijing: Dongfang Chubanshe, 1995.

Yang, Jie. "Reemployment Stars: Language, Gender and Neoliberal Restructuring in China." In *Words, Worlds, and Material Girls: Language, Gender, Globalization,* edited by Bonnie S. McElhinny, 73–102. Berlin: Mouton De Gruyter, 2007.

———. "The Crisis of Masculinity: Class, Gender, and Kindly Power in Post-Mao China." *American Ethnologist* 37, no. 3 (2010): 550–62.

Yang Zhihua. "Qinjian jianguo qinjian chijia wei shehui zhuyi jianshe gengda de Liliang" (Thrifty for the country and the family, contributing more to socialist construction). *Renmin ribao,* June 5, 1957.

———. "Xuyan." (Preface.) In *Da Yuejin zhong de zhigong jiashu* (Dependents in the Great Leap Forward), edited by All-China Federation of Trade Union's Women Worker Council and All-China Women's Federation's Propaganda Office, 1–2. Beijing: Gongren Chubanshe, 1960.

Ying Da, Lü Xiaopin, and Ying Ning. *Dongbei yijiaren* (A family in the northeast). *Chinese Central Television.* 2001.

Yngvesson, Barbara. *Virtuous Citizens, Disruptive Subjects: Order and Complaint in a New England Court.* New York: Routledge, 1993.

Yuan Shuyi and Dong Conglin. *Jindai Zhongguo xiaonong jingji de bianqian* (Transformation of the petty peasantry economy in contemporary China) Beijing: Renmin Chubanshe, 2001.

Zachmann, Karin. "A Socialist Consumption Junction: Debating the Mechanization of Housework in East Germany, 1956–1957." *Technology and Culture* 43, no. 1 (2002): 73–99.

Zhang Meng. *Erduo da you fu* (Lucky dog). DVD. Zhongguo Dianying Jituan Gongsi and Beijing Zijincheng Sanlian Yingshi Faxing Youxian Gongsi. 2008.

Zhang, Qian Forrest, Carlos Oya, and Jingzhong Ye. "Bringing Agriculture Back In: The Central Place of Agrarian Change in Rural China Studies." *Journal of Agrarian Change* 15, no. 3 (2015): 299–313.

Zhang Youyi. "Benshiji ersanshi niandai woguo diquan fenpei de zaiguji" (A reestimation of land ownership distribution in China in the 1920s and 1930s). *Zhongguo shehui jingjishi yanjiu* (Chinese Socio-economic Historical Studies) no. 2 (1988): 3–10.

Zhong Xueping, and Ming Ren. "'Funü neng ding banbiantian': Yige you sizhong shuofa de gushi" (Four interpretations of the slogan "Women hold up half the sky") *Nankai xuebao* (Nankai journal), no. 4 (2009): 54–64.

"Zhonghua Quanguo Zonggonghui zhaokai Quanguo Zhigong Jiashu Gongzuo Huiyi, jueding jiaqiang zhigong jiashu gongzuo" (All-China Federation of Trade Unions organized National Dependent Workers' Congress decided to enhance work related to dependents). *Renmin ribao*, November 14, 1951.

Zhou, Shengxian. *Chongman xiwang de shinian–xinshiqi Zhongguo linye kuayueshi fazhan guihua* (A decade of hope: The leaping-across-style development plan for China's forestry industry in the new century). Beijing: Zhongguo Linye Chubanshe, 2001.

Zhou Shuxuan. "Danwei zhidu zhuanbian dui nüxing de yingxiang" (The impacts of work-unit transformation on Chinese women)." *Zhongguo jiti jingji* no. 8 (2009): 199–200.

Zhu, Jiangang. "Not against the State, Just Protecting Residents' Interests: An Urban Movement in a Shanghai Neighborhood." In *China's Embedded Activism: Opportunities and Constraints of a Social Movement*, edited by Peter Ho and Richard Louis Edmonds, 151–70. London: Routledge Taylor & Francis, 2008.

Zong, Yongqiang, and Xiqing Chen. "The 1998 Flood on the Yangtze, China." *Natural Hazard* 22 (2000): 165–84.

INDEX

Page references in *italics* indicate photos or other illustrations.

Central Committee (CCP), 45, 110, 153n5, 153–54n8
central planning, 85, 87
Cheer Up, ix
Chen Meimei, 134
childcare, 8, 30, 42, 44, 56, 58
China fir (*Cunninghamia*), 39, 66, 140, 150n1
Chinese Central Television Lunar New Year Gala, ix
Chinese Communist Party (CCP), ix, 5, 19, 23, 46, 64, 76, 99, 103, 101, 108; family crisis and, 47; forestry and, 66; new society and, 104
Chinese red pine (*Pinus tabuliformis*), 39, 66, 140, 150n1
Chinese State Council, 153n5
Chinese stock market, rise of, 90–91
Civil Rights Act (US, 1964), Title VII of, 158n3
class struggle, 3, 11, 93, 124; practice, 101; state-endorsed, 100
clear-cutting, corporatization and, 83–92
clothing, 31, 56, 57, 58, 72, 148n17
collective enterprises, 86, 121, 129, 135; assets of, 118; first-generation, 81; land/asset sales from, 125; privatization of, 88; sawmill-affiliated, 81; state-enterprise-affiliated, 80
collective workers, 10, 14, 86, 90, 119–25, 130–31; classification of, 121; female, 82–83, 84; identity/legal standing of, 120; layoffs of, 126; privatization and, 136; protests by, 115; second-generation, 11; stories of, 133, 135, 136, 137, 144; women, 78, 120, 124
collective workshops, 81–82, 83
collectives, 51; rural, 25, 45; village, 65
collectivization, 6, 8, 100, 128, 143; rural,

151n5; socialist, xi, 45
colonialism, 10, 38, 39
Communist Youth League, 20, 50
compensation, 69, 120; individual, 84; performance-based, 84
"Cong zhangxian dao xiaoshi" (Song), 152n26
conservation, 2; forest, 7, 66, 75, 140
consumerism, 19, 56, 114
Contesting Citizenship (Solinger), 149n3
cooperatives: advanced, 26; elementary, 26; employee-owned, 86; rural, 42; village, 26
corruption, 104, 130; campaign against, 131; equity and, 33
COVID-19, 145, 155n5
cultural environment, 62, 64, 76, 102
Cultural Revolution (1966–76), 3, 79–80, 88, 114
culture, ix, 76, 112; forests and, 62–65

danwei, 8, 30, 34, 36, 43; design of, 31; infrastructure of, 150n11; management system, 156n19; political mechanism of, 33; rural/urban, 37. *See also* work units
day care centers, 30. *See also* childcare
"Decision on Accelerating Forestry Development," 148n15
"Decision on Institutional Reform of the Enterprise Employees' Retirement Insurance," 109
deforestation, 66, 67, 141, 154n13
DeGraffenreid v. General Motors Assembly Division, St. Louis (1976), 158n3
demonstrations. *See* protests
Deng Xiaoping, 3, 83, 155n7
Department of Forestry, 136–37
dependent workers, 41, 44, 53, 109; em-

sawmill workers, 2, 33, 83, 88, 106; female, 89, 101–2; first-generation, 80; interviews of, 77

scar literature, 114

segregation, urban-rural, 9, 25

severance pay, 10, 120, 125. *See also* income; pensions

Shandong, 18, 21–25, 29, 33, 38, 41; migrants to, 39

Shanghai, 24, 25, 29, 33, 66, 67

Shaowu, 1, 7, 10, 17, 22–23, 29; activism in, 126; employment in, 70; interviews in, 77; peasants in, 70; reconnecting with, 145; state forest farms in, 27–28; traveling to, 79, 80, 139; work units in, 31

Shaowu City Court, Forestry Department and, 137

Shaowu City Hall, gathering at, 117

Shaowu Sawmill, 1, 34, 56, 65, 81, 82; assets of, 122; demolition of, 17; gender differences at, 42; history of, 121–22; interviews at, x; living at, 50, 51; map of, 32; privatization of, 88, 119; processing/sale/transportation and, 28; social security and, 122; state enterprise of, 130; workers from, 2, 30, 117, 120; workshops at, 83

slaves, reproduction by, 153, 153n41

social needs, 8, 47

social networks, 88, 143, 145

social reproduction, 33, 43, 148n4

social security, 84, 89, 92, 109, 122

Social Security Bureau, 131

social status, 9, 125

social welfare, 84

socialism, xii, 10, 11, 37, 38, 58, 128; building, 45; capital accumulation and, 14; capitalism and, 15; legacy of, 129; radical, 124; state capitalism and, 3–4

socialist development, 18, 38, 45, 55, 59, 102

socialist economy, 26, 44, 46, 58, 87, 94

Societies of Senior Citizens (SSC), 132

Solinger, Dorothy, 149n3

Song dynasty, 152n26, 152n29

Song Qingling, 44

speaking bitterness, 110; described, 100; impact of, 109, 111; long-term, 115; in Maoist campaigns, 99–102; meetings, 100; narrative, 101–2, 104; party-state and, 108; practice of, 14–15; protests and, 112–13; as slow-acting poison, 111; *waipo* and, 102–9

"Start Over," ix

state capitalism, xii, 114, 128, 142; disruption of, 135; labor exploitation under, 3; socialism and, 3–4, 6, 13; transformation into, 5, 14. *See also* capitalism

State Council, 109, 148n15, 154n8

state enterprises, 7, 38, 86, 87, 92, 93, 105, 106; collective enterprises and, 80; development of, 119, 122; privatization of, 108

state forestry, 2, 14, 25–26, 38, 39, 113; establishing, 5–6, 21; rations for, 49; transition for, 140; work/life in, 28–31, 33–34, 36–37, 143

state socialism, 5; state capitalism and, 6, 13

state workers, 11, 13, 80, 86, 105, 122; entry-level, 81; female, 107; first-generation, 120; income for, 83, 84; layoff of, 89, 120, 131, 144; male, 81–82; means of production and, 96; rations for, 49; retired, 144

storytelling, 13, 114, 140, 144

structural oppression, 140, 142, 144

Taishi Village, 127, 133